Modern Critical Interpretations

Exodus

Modern Critical Interpretations

These and other titles in preparation

Modern Critical Interpretations

Exodus

Edited and with an introduction by

Harold Bloom
Sterling Professor of the Humanities
Yale University

Chelsea House Publishers ◊ *1987*
NEW YORK ◊ NEW HAVEN ◊ PHILADELPHIA

© 1987 by Chelsea House Publishers, a division
of Chelsea House Educational Communications, Inc.,
  95 Madison Avenue, New York, NY 10016
  345 Whitney Avenue, New Haven, CT 06511
  5068B West Chester Pike, Edgemont, PA 19028

Introduction © 1987 by Harold Bloom

Printed and bound in the United States of America

10   9   8   7   6   5   4   3   2   1

∞ The paper used in this publication meets the minimum
requirements of the American National Standard for Permanence
of Paper for Printed Library Materials, Z39.48-1984.

Library of Congress Cataloging-in-Publication Data
Exodus.
   (Modern critical interpretations)
   Bibliography: p.
   Includes index.
   Contents: Moses an Egyptian / Sigmund Freud—the
burning bush; Holy event / Martin Buber—Exodus 1–4.
the prologue to the Exodus cycle / Michael Fishbane—
[etc.]
   1. Bible. O.T. Exodus—Criticism, interpretation,
ets. 2. Bible as literatur. 3. Bible. OT. Exodus—
Language, style. I. Bloom, Harold. II. Series.
BS1245.2.E94   1987   222'.12066   87–11668
ISBN 0–87754–909–5 (pbk.)

Contents

Editor's Note

This book brings together a representative selection of what I judge to be the best modern literary interpretations of Exodus, the second book of the Hebrew and Christian Bible. The critical essays are reprinted here in the chronological order of their original publication. I am grateful to Hillary Kelleher for her aid in editing this volume.

My introduction centers upon the J writer, author of the oldest narrative strand in Genesis, Exodus, and Numbers, and traces his vision of Yahweh until its culmination in the Sinai theophany in Exodus.

Sigmund Freud, founder of psychoanalysis, leads off the chronological sequence with the audacious speculation that begins his late fiction, *Moses and Monotheism*. In the pattern of Freud's own *Totem and Taboo,* we are given the extraordinary projection of Moses as an Egyptian, slain by the Israelites whom he led, and afterwards worshipped by them as a kind of ancestor god.

A very different thinker, Martin Buber, seer of the dialogue between I and Thou, follows with two of his fervent interpretations of Exodus, one centering on the Burning Bush, and the other on the "Holy Event" of the Mosaic Covenant.

The literary structure of the first four chapters of Exodus is analyzed by Michael Fishbane, after which Northrop Frye, our foremost anatomist of literary criticism, studies Exodus as the narrative myth of deliverance.

Michael Walzer, writing from the perspective of political philosophy, finds in the Exodus vision of Egypt the perpetual paradigm of revolutionary defeat. The triumphal Song of the Sea or Song of Moses receives an acute exegesis from Robert Alter, a pioneer in the study of the art of biblical poetry and narrative.

This book concludes with Leslie Brisman's essay on the Divine Presence in Exodus, published here for the first time. Brisman's distinguished rejuvenation of normative tradition into a mode of literary analysis contrasts sharply with my introduction, with its insistence that the Yahwist's vision of God and the normative tradition's vision cannot be reconciled.

Introduction

The Great Original of the literary and oral traditions that merged into normative Judaism was the writer scholarly convention rather wonderfully chose to call "J." Since Kafka is the most legitimate descendant of one aspect of the antithetical J (Tolstoy and the early, pre-Coleridgean Wordsworth are the most authentic descendants of J's other side), I find it useful to adopt the formula "from J to K," in order to describe the uncanny or antithetical elements in J's narratives. The J who could have written *Hadji Murad* or *The Tale of Margaret* was the inevitable fountainhead of what eventually became normative Judaism. But this first, strongest, and still somehow most Jewish of all our writers also could have written "The Hunger Gracchus" or even "Josephine the Singer and the Mouse Folk." Indeed he wrote uncannier stories than Kafka lived to write. How those stories ever could have been acceptable or even comprehensible to the P authors or the Deuteronomist, to the Academy of Ezra or the Pharisees, let alone to Akiba and his colleagues, is a mystery that I have been trying to clarify by developing a critical concept of what I call "facticity," a kind of brute contingency by which an author's strength blinds and incarcerates a tradition of belated readership. But here I primarily want to describe the uncanniness of J's work, so as to break out of facticity, insofar as I am able to do so.

But "the uncanny" I mean Freud's concept, since that appears to be the authentic modern version of what once was called the Sublime. Freud defines "the uncanny" as being "in reality nothing new or foreign, but something familiar and old-established in the mind that has been estranged only by the process of repression." Since I myself, as a critic, am obsessed with the Sublime or Freud's "uncanny," I realize that my reading of any Sublime work or fragment is always dependent upon an estrangement, in which the repressed returns upon me to end that estrangement, but only momentarily. The uncanniness of the Yahwist exceeds that of all other writers, because in him both the estrangement and the return achieve maximum force.

Of course J himself is considered to be a fiction, variously referred to by scholars as a school, a tradition, a document, and a hypothesis. Well, Homer is perhaps a fiction too, and these days the slaves of critical fashion do not weary of proclaiming the death of the author, or at least the reduction of every author to the status of a Nietzschean fiction. But J is pragmatically the author-of-authors, in that his authority and originality constitute a difference that has made a difference. The teller of the tales of Jacob and of Joseph, of Moses and the Exodus, is a writer more inescapable than Shakespeare and more pervasive in our consciousness than Freud. J's only cultural rival would be an unlikely compound of Homer and Plato. Plato's contest with Homer seems to me to mark one of the largest differences between the ancient Greeks and the Hebrews. The agon for the mind of Athens found no equivalent in Jerusalem, and so the Yahwist still remains the mind of Jerusalem, everywhere that Jerusalem happens to be.

I do not believe that J was a fiction, and indeed J troubles me because his uncanniness calls into question my own conviction that every writer is belated, and so is always an inter-poet. J's freedom from belatedness rivals Shakespeare's, which is to say that J's originality is as intense as Shakespeare's. But J wrote twenty-five hundred years before Shakespeare, and that time-span bewilders comparison. I am going to sketch J's possible circumstances and purposes, in order to hazard a description of J's tone or of the uncanniness of his stance as a writer. Not much in my sketch will flout received scholarship, but necessarily I will have to go beyond the present state of biblical scholarship, since it cannot even decide precisely which texts are J's, or even revised by others from J. My attempt at transcending scholarship is simply a literary critic's final reliance upon her or his own sense of a text, or what I have called the necessity of misreading. No critic, whatever her or his moldiness *or* skepticism, can evade a Nietzschean will to power over a text, because interpretation is at last nothing else. The text, even if it was written that morning, and shown by its poet to the critic at high noon, is already lost in time, as lost as the Yahwist. Time says, "It was," and authentic criticism, as Nietzsche implied, is necessarily pervaded by a will for revenge against time's "it was." No interpreter can suspend the will to relational knowledge for more than an isolated moment, and since all narrative and all poetry are also interpretation, all writing manifests such a will.

Solomon the King, nowhere of course overtly mentioned by J, is the dominant contemporary force in the context of J's writing. I would go further, and as a pious Stevensian would say that Solomon is J's motive for metaphor. The reign of Solomon ended in the year 922 before the Common Era, and J quite possibly wrote either in Solomon's last years, or—more likely, I think—shortly thereafter. One can venture that Solomon was to J what Elizabeth was to Shakespeare, an idea of order, as crucial in J's Jerusalem as it was in Shakespeare's London. The Imperial Theme is J's countersong, though J's main burden is a heroic and agonistic past represented by David the King, while his implied judgment upon the imperial present is at best skeptical, since he implies also an agonistic future. J's vision of agon centers his uncanny stance, accounting for his nearly unique mode of irony.

How much of J's actual text we have lost to the replacement tactics of redactors we cannot know, but biblical scholarship has not persuaded me that either the so-called Elohistic or the Priestly redactors provide fully coherent visions of their own, except perhaps for the Priestly first chapter of Genesis, which is so startling a contrast to J's account of how we all got started. But let me sketch the main contours of J's narrative, as we appear to have it. Yahweh begins his Creation in the first harsh Judean spring, before the first rain comes down. Water wells up from the earth, and Yahweh molds Adam out of the red clay, breathing into the earthling's nostrils a breath of the divine life. Then come the stories we think we know: Eve, the serpent, Cain and Abel, Seth, Noah and the Flood, the tower of Babel, and something utterly new with Abraham. From Abraham on, the main sequence again belongs to J: the Covenant, Ishmael, Yahweh at Mamre and on the road to Sodom, Lot, Isaac and the Akedah, Rebecca, Esau and Jacob, the tales of Jacob, Tamar, the story of Joseph and his brothers, and then the Mosaic account. Moses, so far as I can tell, meant much less to J than he did to the normative redactors, and so the J strand in Exodus and Numbers is even more laconic than J tended to be earlier.

In J's Exodus we find the oppression of the Jews, the birth of Moses, his escape to Midian, the burning bush and the instruction, the weird murderous attack by Yahweh upon Moses, the audiences with

Pharaoh, the plagues, and the departure, flight, and crossing. Matters become sparser with Israel in the wilderness, at the Sinai covenant, and then with the dissensions and the battles in Numbers. J flares up finally on a grand scale in the serio-comic Balaam and Balak episode, but that is not the end of J's work, even as we have it. The Deuteronomist memorably incorporates J in his chapters 31 and 34 dealing with the death of Moses. I give here in sequence the opening and the closing of what we hear J's Yahweh speaking aloud, first to Adam and last to Moses: "Of every tree in the garden you are free to eat; but as for the tree of knowledge of good and bad, you must not eat of it; for as soon as you eat of it, you shall die." "This is the land of which I swore to Abraham, Isaac, and Jacob, 'I will give it to your offspring.' I have let you see it with your own eyes, but you shall not cross there." Rhetorically, the two speeches share the same cruel pattern of power: "Here it is; it is yours and yet it is not yours." Akin to J's counterpointing of Yahweh's first and last speeches is his counterparting of Yahweh's first and last actions: "Yahweh formed man from the dust of the earth," and "Yahweh buried him, Moses, in the valley of the land of Moab, near Beth-peor; and no one knows his burial place to this day." From Adam to Moses is from earth to earth; Yahweh molds us and he buries us, and both actions are done with his own hands. As it was with Adam and Moses, so it was with David and with Solomon, and with those who come and will come after Solomon. J is the harshest and most monitory of writers, and his Yahweh is an uncanny god, who takes away much of what he gives, and who is beyond any standard of measurement. And yet what I have said about J so far is not even part of the truth; isolated, all by itself, it is not true at all, for J is a writer who exalts man, and who has most peculiar relations with God. Gorky once said to Tolstoy that Tolstoy's relation to God reminded him of the Russian proverb "Two bears in one den." J's relation of his uncanny Yahweh frequently reminds me of my favorite Yiddish apothegm: "Sleep faster, we need the pillows." J barely can keep up with Yahweh, though J's Jacob almost can, while J's Moses cannot keep up at all. Since what is most problematic about J's writing is Yahweh, I suggest we take a closer look at J's Yahweh than the entire normative and modern scholarly tradition has been willing or able to take. Homer and Dante, Shakespeare and Milton, hardly lacked audacity in representing what may be beyond representation, but J was both bolder and shrewder than any other writer at inventing speeches and actions for God Himself. Only J convinces us that he knows precisely how and when Yahweh speaks; Isaiah compares poorly to J in this, while the Milton of *Paradise Lost,* book 3, hardly rates even as an involuntary parodist of J.

I am moved to ask a question which the normative tradition— Judaic, Christian, and even secular—cannot ask: What is J's stance toward Yahweh? I can begin an answer by listing all that it is not: creating Yahweh, J's primary emotions do not include awe, fear, wonder, much surprise, or even love. J *sounds* rather matter-of-fact, but that is part of J's unique mode of irony. By turns, J's stance toward Yahweh is appreciative, wryly apprehensive, intensely interested, and above all attentive and alert. Toward Yahweh, J is perhaps a touch wary; J is always *prepared to be surprised.* What J knows is that Yahweh is Sublime or "uncanny," incommensurate yet rather agonistic, curious and lively, humorous yet irascible, and all too capable of suddenly violent action. But J's Yahweh is rather *heimlich* also; he sensibly avoids walking about in the Near Eastern heat, preferring the cool of the evening, and he likes to sit under the terebinths at Mamre, devouring roast calf and curds. J would have laughed at his normative descendants—Christian, Jewish, secular, scholarly—who go on calling his representations of Yahweh "anthropomorphic," when they should be calling his representations of Jacob "theomorphic."

"The anthropomorphic" always has been a misleading concept, and probably was the largest single element affecting the long history of the redaction of J that evolved into normative Judaism. Most modern scholars, Jewish and Gentile alike, cannot seem to accept the fact that there was no Jewish theology before Philo. "Jewish theology," despite its long history from Philo to Franz Rosenzweig, is therefore an oxymoron, particularly when applied to biblical texts, and most particularly when applied to J. J's Yahweh is an uncanny personality, and not at all a concept. Yahweh sometimes *seems* to behave like us, but because Yahweh and his sculpted creature, Adam, are incommensurate, this remains a mere seeming. Sometimes, and always within limits, we behave like Yahweh, and not necessarily because we will to do so. There is a true sense in which John Calvin was as strong a reader of J as he more clearly was of Job, a sense displayed in the paradox of the Protestant Yahweh who entraps his believers by an impossible double injunction, which might be phrased: "Be like me, but don't you dare to be too like me!" In J, the paradox emerges only gradually, and does not reach its climax until the theophany on Sinai. Until Sinai, J's Yahweh addresses himself only to a handful, to his elite: Adam, Noah, Abraham, Jacob, Joseph, and, by profound implication, David. But at Sinai, we encounter the crisis of J's writing, as we will see.

What is theomorphic about Adam, Noah, Abraham, Jacob, Joseph? I think the question should be rephrased: What is Davidic about them? About Joseph, everything, and indeed J's Joseph I read as a fictive representation of David, rather in the way Virgil's Divine Child represents Augustus, except that J is working on a grand scale with Joseph, bringing to perfection what may have been an old mode of romance.

I have called Solomon J's motive for metaphor, but that calling resounds with Nietzsche's motive for all trope: the desire to be different, the desire to be elsewhere. For J, the difference, the elsewhere, is David. J's agonistic elitism, the struggle for the blessing, is represented by Abraham, above all by Jacob, and by Tamar also. But the bearer of the blessing is David, and I have ventured the surmise that J's Joseph is a portrait of David. Though this surmise is, I think, original, the centering of J's humanism upon the implied figure of David is not, of course, original with me. It is a fundamental postulate of the school of Gerhard von Rad, worked out in detail by theologians like Hans Walter Wolff and Walter Brueggemann. Still, a phrase like Wolff's "the Kerygma of the Yahwist" makes me rather uneasy, since J is no more a theologian than he is a priest or prophet. Freud, like St. Paul, has a message, but J, like Shakespeare, does not. J *is* literature and not "confession," which of course is not true of his redactors. They were on the road to Akiba, but J, always in excess of the normative, was no quester.

I find no traces of cult in J, and I am puzzled that so many read as kerygmatic Yahweh's words to Abram in Gen. 12:3: "So, then, all the families of the earth can gain a blessing in you." The blessing, in J, simply does not mean what it came to mean in his redactors and in the subsequent normative tradition. To gain a blessing, particularly through the blessing that becomes Abraham's, is in J to join oneself to that elitist agon which culminated in the figure of the agonistic hero, David. To be blessed means ultimately that one's name will not be scattered, and the remembered name will retain life into a time without boundaries. The blessing then is temporal, and not spatial, as it was in Homer and in the Greeks after him, who like his heroes struggled for the foremost place. And a temporal blessing, like the kingdom in Shakespeare, finds its problematic aspect in the vicissitudes of descendants.

Jacob is J's central man, whose fruition, deferred in the beloved

Joseph, because given to Judah, has come just before J's time in the triumph of David. I think that Brueggemann is imaginatively accurate in his hypothesis that David represented, for J, a new kind of man, almost a new Adam, the man whom Yahweh (in 2 Sam. 7) had decided to trust. Doubtless we cannot exclude from our considerations the messianic tradition that the normative, Jewish and Christian, were to draw out from those two great contemporary writers, J and the author of 2 Samuel. But J does not have any such messianic consciousness about David. Quite the reverse: for him, we can surmise, David had been and was the elite *image:* not a harbinger of a greater vision to come, but a fully human being who already had exhausted the full range and vitality of man's possibilities. If, as Brueggemann speculates, J's tropes of exile (Gen. 3:24; 4:12; 11:8) represent the true images of the Solomonic present, then I would find J's prime Davidic trope in Jacob's return to Canaan, marked by the all-night, all-in wrestling match that concentrates Jacob's name forever as Israel. The Davidic glory then is felt most strongly in Jacob's theomorphic triumph, rendered so much the more poignant by his permanent crippling: "The sun rose upon him as he passed Penuel, limping on his hip."

If Jacob is Israel as the father, then David, through the trope of Joseph, is Jacob's or Israel's truest son. What then is Davidic about J's Jacob? I like the late E. A. Speiser's surmise that J personally knew his great contemporary, the writer who gave us, in 2 Samuel, the history of David and his immediate successors. J's Joseph reads to me like a lovingly ironic parody of the David of the court historian. What matters most about David, as that model narrative presents him, is not only his charismatic intensity, but the marvelous gratuity of Yahweh's *hesed,* his Election-love for this most heroic of his favorites. To no one in J's text does Yahweh speak so undialectically as he does through Nathan to David in 2 Sam. 7:12–16:

> When your days are done and you lie with your fathers, I
> will raise up your offspring after you, one of your own
> issue, and I will establish his kingship. He shall build a
> house for My name, and I will establish his royal throne
> forever. I will be a father to him, and he shall be a son to
> Me. When he does wrong, I will chastise him with the rod
> of men and the affliction of mortals; but I will never with-
> draw My favor from him as I withdrew it from Saul, whom
> I removed to make room for you. Your house and your

kingship shall ever be secure before you; your throne shall
be established forever.

The blessing in J, as I have written elsewhere, is always agonistic,
and Jacob is J's supreme agonist. But J makes a single exception for
Joseph, and clearly with the reader's eye centered upon David. From
the womb on to the ford of the Jabbok, Jacob is an agonist, and until
that night encounter at Penuel by no means a heroic one. His agon, as
I've said, is for the temporal blessing that will prevail into a time
without boundaries; and so it never resembles the Homeric or the
Athenian contest for the foremost place, a kind of topological or spatial
blessing. In J, the struggle is for the uncanny gift of life, for the breath
of Yahweh that transforms *adamah* into Adam. True, David struggles,
and suffers, but J's Joseph serenely voyages through all vicissitudes,
as though J were intimating that David's agon had been of a new
kind, one in which the obligation was wholly and voluntarily on
Yahweh's side of the Covenant. Jacob the father wrestles lifelong, and
is permanently crippled by the climactic match with a nameless one
among the Elohim whom I interpret as the baffled angel of death, who
learns that Israel lives, and always will survive. Joseph the son charms
reality, even as David seems to have charmed Yahweh.

But Jacob, I surmise, was J's signature, and while the portrait of
the Davidic Joseph manifests J's wistfulness, the representation of
Jacob may well be J's self-portrait as the great writer of Israel. My
earlier question would then become: What is Davidic about J himself,
not as a person perhaps, but certainly as an author? My first observa-
tion here would have to be this apparent paradox: J is anything but a
religious writer, unlike all his revisionists and interpreters, and David
is anything but a religious personality, despite having become the
paradigm for all messianic speculation, both Jewish and Christian.
Again I am in the wake of von Rad and his school, but with this
crucial Bloomian swerve: J and David are not religious, just as Freud,
for all his avowedly antireligious polemic, is finally nothing but religious. Freud's overdetermination of meaning, his emphasis upon primal repression or a flight from representation—before, indeed, there
was anything to represent—establishes Freud as normatively Jewish
despite himself. Turn it and turn it, for everything is in it, the sage ben
Bag Bag said of Torah, and Freud says the same of the psyche. If there
is sense in everything, then everything that is going to happen has
happened already, and so reality is already in the past and there never

can be anything new. Freud's stance toward psychic history is the normative rabbinical stance toward Jewish history, and if Akiba is the paradigm for what it is to be religious, then the professedly scientistic Freud is as religious as Akiba, if we are speaking of the Jewish religion. But J, like the court historian's David of 2 Samuel, is quite Jewish without being at all religious, in the belated normative sense. For the uncanny J and for the path-breaking David, everything that matters most is perpetually new.

But this is true of J's Jacob also, as it is of Abraham, even Isaac, and certainly Tamar—all live at the edge of life rushing onwards, never in a static present but always in the dynamism of J's Yahweh, whose incessant temporality generates anxious expectations in nearly every fresh sentence of certain passages. This is again the Kafkan aspect of J, though it is offset by J's strong sense of human freedom, a sense surpassing its Homeric parallels. What becomes theodicy in J's revisionists down to Milton is for J not at all a perplexity. Since J has no concept of Yahweh but rather a sense of Yahweh's peculiar personality, the interventions of Yahweh in primal family history do not impinge upon his elite's individual freedom. So we have the memorable and grimly funny argument between Yahweh and Abraham as they walk together down the road to Sodom. Abraham wears Yahweh down until Yahweh quite properly begins to get exasperated. The shrewd courage and humanity of Abraham convince me that in the Akedah the redactors simply eliminated J's text almost completely. As I read the Hebrew, there is an extraordinary gap between the Elohistic language and the sublime invention of the story. J's Abraham would have argued far more tenaciously with Yahweh for his son's life than he did in defense of the inhabitants of the sinful cities of the plain, and here the redactionists may have defrauded us of J's uncanny greatness at its height.

But how much they *have* left us which the normative tradition has been incapable of assimilating! I think the best way of seeing this is to juxtapose with J the Pharasaic Book of Jubilees, oddly called also "the Little Genesis," though it is prolix and redundant in every tiresome way. Written about one hundred years before the Common Era, Jubilees is a normative travesty of Genesis, far more severely, say, than Chronicles is a normative reduction of 2 Samuel. But though he writes so boringly, what is wonderfully illuminating about the author of Jubilees is that he totally eradicates J's text. Had he set out deliberately to remove everything idiosyncratic about J's share in Torah, he could have done no more thorough a job. Gone altogether is J's creation story of Yahweh molding the red clay into Adam and then breathing life into his own image. Gone as well is Yahweh at Mamre, where only angels now appear to Abraham and Sarah, and there is no dispute on the road to Sodom. And the Satanic prince of angels, Mastema, instigates Yahweh's trial of Abraham in the Akedah. Jacob and Esau do not wrestle in the womb, and Abraham prefers Jacob, though even the author of Jubilees does not go so far as to deny Isaac's greater love for Esau. Gone, alas totally gone, is J's sublime invention of the night wrestling at Penuel. Joseph lacks all charm and mischief, necessarily, and the agony of Jacob, and the subsequent grandeur of the reunion, are vanished away. Most revealingly, the uncanniest moment in J, Yahweh's attempt to murder Moses en route to Egypt, becomes Mastema's act. And wholly absent is J's most enigmatic vision, the Sinai theophany, which is replaced by the safe removal of J's too-lively Yahweh back to a sedate dwelling in the high heavens.

II

J's originality was too radical to be absorbed, and yet abides even now as the originality of a Yahweh who will not dwindle down into the normative Godhead of the Jews, Christians, and Muslims. Because J cared more for personality than for morality, and cared not at all for cult, his legacy is a disturbing sense that, as Blake phrased it, forms of worship have been chosen from poetic tales. J was no theologian and yet not a maker of saga or epic, and again not a historian, and not even a storyteller as such. We have no description of J that will fit, just as we have no idea of God that will contain his irrepressible Yahweh. I want to test these observations by a careful account of J's Sinai theophany, where his Yahweh is more problematic than scholarship has been willing to perceive.

Despite the truncation, indeed the possible mutilation of J's account of the Sinai theophany, more than enough remains to mark it as the crisis or crossing-point of his work. For the first time, his Yahweh is overwhelmingly self-contradictory, rather than dialectical, ironic, or even crafty. The moment of crisis turns upon Yahweh's confrontation with the Israelite host. Is he to allow himself to be seen by them? How direct is his self-representation to be? Mamre and the road to Sodom suddenly seem estranged, or as though they never were. It is not that here Yahweh is presented less anthropomorphically, but that J's Moses (let alone those he leads) is far less theomorphic or Davidic than J's

Abraham and J's Jacob, and certainly less theomorphic or Davidic than J's Joseph. Confronting his agonistic and theomorphic elite, from Abraham to the implied presence of David, Yahweh is both canny and uncanny. But Moses is neither theomorphic nor agonistic. J's Sinai theophany marks the moment of the blessing's transition from the elite to the entire Israelite host, and in that transition a true anxiety of representation breaks forth in J's work for the first time.

I follow Martin Noth's lead, in the main, as to those passages in Exodus 19 and 24 that are clearly J's, though my ear accepts as likely certain moments he considers only probable or at least quite possible. Here are Exod. 19:9–15, 18, 20–25, literally rendered:

> Yahweh said to Moses: "I will come to you in a thick cloud, that the people may hear that I speak with you and that they may trust you forever afterwards." Moses then reported the people's words to Yahweh, and Yahweh said to Moses: "Go to the people and warn them to be continent today and tomorrow. Let them wash their clothes. Let them be pre-pared for the third day, for on the third day Yahweh will descend upon Mount Sinai, in the sight of all the people. You shall set limits for the people all around, saying: 'Be-ware of climbing the mountain or touching the border of it. Whoever touches the mountain shall be put to death; no hand shall touch him, but either he shall be stoned or shot; whether beast or man, he shall not live.' When there is a loud blast of the ram's horn, then they may ascend the mountain."
>
> Moses came down from the mountain unto the people and warned them to remain pure, and they washed their clothes. And Moses said to the people: "Prepare for the third day; do not approach a woman."

Yahweh will come at first in a thick cloud, that the people may hear yet presumably not see him; nevertheless, on the third day he will come down upon Sinai "in the sight of all the people." Sinai will be taboo, but is this only a taboo of touch? What about seeing Yahweh? I suspect that an ellipsis, wholly characteristic of J's rhetorical strength, then intervened, again characteristically filled in by the E redactors as verses 16 and 17, and again as verse 19; but in verse 18 clearly we hear J's grand tone:

> Now Mount Sinai was all in smoke, for the Lord had come
> down upon it in fire; the smoke rose like the smoke of a
> kiln, and all the people trembled violently.

Whether people or mountain tremble hardly matters in this great trope of immanent power. Yahweh, as we know, is neither the fire nor in the fire, for the ultimate trope is the *makom:* Yahweh is the place of the world, but the world is not his place, and so Yahweh is also the place of the fire, but the fire is not his place. And so J touches the heights of his own Sublime, though himself troubled by an anxiety of representation previously unknown to him, an anxiety of touch and, for the first time, of sight:

> Yahweh came down upon Mount Sinai, on the mountain
> top, and Yahweh called Moses to the mountain top, and
> Moses went up. Yahweh said to Moses: "Go down, warn
> the people not to break through to gaze at Yahweh, lest
> many of them die. And the priests who come near Yahweh
> must purify themselves, lest Yahweh break forth against
> them." But Moses said to Yahweh: "The people cannot
> come up to Mount Sinai, for You warned us when You
> said: 'Set limits about the mountain and render it holy.' "So
> Yahweh said to Moses: "Go down and come back with
> Aaron, but do not allow the priests or the people to break
> through to come up to Yahweh, lest Yahweh break out
> against them." And Moses descended to the people and
> spoke to them.

However much we have grown accustomed to J, he has not prepared us for this. Never before has Yahweh, bent upon Covenant, been a potential catastrophe as well as a potential blessing. But then, certainly the difference is in the movement from an elite to a whole people. If, as I suspect, the pragmatic covenant for J was the Davidic or humanistic or theomorphic covenant, then the most salient poetic meaning here was contemporary, whether Solomonic or just after. The true covenant, without anxiety or the problematic of representation, was agonistic: with Abraham, with Jacob, with Joseph, with David, but neither with Moses nor with Solomon, and so never with the mass of the people, whether at Sinai or at J's own moment of writing. J is as elitist as Shakespeare, or as Freud; none of the three was exactly a writer on the left. Yahweh himself, in J's vision, becomes dangerously confused in the anxious expectations of at once favoring and threatening the host of the people, rather than the individuals, that he has chosen. When Moses reminds Yahweh that Sinai is off-limits anyway, Yahweh evidently is too preoccupied and too little taken with Moses even to listen, and merely repeats his warning that he may be uncontrollable, even by himself.

As our text now stands, the revisionists take over, and the Commandments are promulgated. I surmise that in J's original text the Commandments, however phrased, came *after* some fragments by J that we still have in what is now Exodus 24:

> Then Yahweh said to Moses: "Come up to Yahweh, with Aaron, Nadab and Abihu, and seventy elders of Israel, and bow low but from afar. And only Moses shall come near Yahweh. The others shall not come near, and the people shall not come up with him at all."
>
> Then Moses and Aaron, Nadab and Abihu, and seventy elders of Israel went up, and they saw the God of Israel; under His feet there was the likeness of a pavement of sapphire, like the very sky for purity. Yet He did not raise His hand against the leaders of the Israelites; they beheld God, and they ate and drank.

This is again J at his uncanniest, the true Western Sublime, and so the truest challenge to a belated Longinian critic like myself. We are at Mamre again, in a sense, except that here the seventy-four who constitute an elite (of sorts) eat and drink, as did the Elohim and Yahweh at Mamre, while now Yahweh watches enigmatically, and (rather wonderfully) is watched. And again, J is proudly self-contradictory, or perhaps even dialectical, his irony being beyond my interpretive ken, whereas his Yahweh is so outrageously self-contradictory that I do not know where precisely to begin in reading the phases of this difference. But rather than enter that labyrinth—of who may or may not see Yahweh, or how, or when—I choose instead to test the one marvelous visual detail against the Second Commandment. Alas, we evidently do not have J's phrasing here, but there is a strength in the diction that may reflect an origin in J:

> You shall not make for yourself a sculptured image, or any likeness of what is in the heavens above, or on the earth below, or in the waters under the earth.

Surely we are to remember J's Yahweh, who formed the *adam* from the dust of the *adamah* and blew into his sculptured image's nostrils the breath of life. The *zelem* is forbidden to us, as our creation. But had it been forbidden to J, at least until now? And even now, does not J make for himself, and so also for us, a likeness of what is in the heavens above? The seventy-four eaters and drinkers saw with their own eyes the God of Israel, and they saw another likeness also: "under His feet there was the likeness of a pavement of sapphire, like the very sky for purity." Why precisely *this* visual image, from this greatest of writers who gives us so very few visual images, as compared to images that are auditory, dynamic, motor urgencies? I take it that J, and not the Hebrew language, inaugurated the extraordinary process of describing any object primarily by telling us not how it looked, but *how it was made*, wonderfully and fearfully made. But here J describes what is seen, not indeed Yahweh in whole or in part, but what we may call Yahweh's chosen stance.

Stance in writing is also tone, and the tone of this passage is crucial but perhaps beyond our determination. Martin Buber, as an eloquent rhetorician, described it with great vividness but with rather too much interpretive confidence in his book, *Moses*. The seventy-four representatives of Israel are personalized by this theorist of dialogical personalism:

> They have presumably wandered through clinging, hanging mist before dawn; and at the very moment they reach their goal, the swaying darkness tears asunder (as I myself happened to witness once) and dissolves except for one cloud already transparent with the hue of the still unrisen sun. The sapphire proximity of the heavens overwhelms the aged shepherds of the Delta, who have never before tasted, who have never been given the slightest idea, of what is shown in the play of early light over the summits of the mountains. And this precisely is perceived by the representatives of the liberated tribes as that which lies under the feet of their enthroned *Melek*.

Always ingenious and here refreshingly naturalistic, Buber nevertheless neglects what he sometimes recognized: J's uncanniness. Buber's motive, as he says, is to combat two opposed yet equally reductive views of biblical theophanies: that they are either supernatural miracles or else impressive fantasies. But had J wanted us to believe that the seventy-four elders of Israel saw only a natural radiance, he would have written rather differently. The commentary of Brevard Childs is very precise: "The text is remarkable for its bluntness: 'They saw the God of Israel.' " Childs adds that from the Septuagint on to Maimonides there is a consistent toning down of the statement's directness. Surely the directness is realized yet more acutely if we recall that this is Yahweh's only appearance in the Hebrew Bible where he *says* absolutely nothing. J's emphasis is clear: the seventy-four are on Sinai to eat and drink in Yahweh's presence, while they stare at him, and he presumably stares right back. But that confronts us with the one visual detail J provides: "under His feet there was the likeness of a pavement of sapphire, like the very sky for purity." J gives us a great trope, which all commentary down to the scholarly present weakly misreads by literalization. J, himself a strong misreader of tradition, demands strong misreadings, and so I venture one here. Let us forget all such notions as Yahweh standing so high up that he seems to stand on the sky, or the old fellows never having seen early light in the mountains before. J is elliptical always; that is crucial to his rhetorical stance. He is too wily to say what you would see, if you sat there in awe, eating and drinking while you saw Yahweh. Indeed, we must assume that Yahweh is sitting, but nothing whatsoever is said about a throne, and J after all is not Isaiah or Micaiah ben Imlah or Ezekiel or John Milton. As at Mamre, Yahweh sits upon the ground, and yet it is as though the sky were beneath his feet. May not this drastic reversal of perspective represent a vertigo of vision on the part of the seventy-four? To see the God of Israel is to see as though the world had been turned upside down. And that indeed Yahweh *is* seen, *contra* Buber, we can know through J's monitory comment: "Yet He did not raise His hand against the leaders of the Israelites; they beheld God, and they ate and drank." The sublimity is balanced *not* by a Covenant meal, as all the scholars solemnly assert, but by a picnic on Sinai.

That this uncanny festivity contradicts Yahweh's earlier warnings is not J's confusion, nor something produced by his redactors, but is a dramatic confusion that J's Yahweh had to manifest if his blessing was to be extended from elite individuals to an entire people. Being incommensurate, Yahweh cannot be said to have thus touched his limits, but in the little more that J wrote Yahweh is rather less lively than he had been. His heart, as J hints, was not with Moses but with David, who was to come. J's heart, I venture as I close, was also not with Moses, nor even with Joseph, as David's surrogate, and not really with Yahweh either. It was with Jacob at the Jabbok, obdurately confronting death in the shape of a time-obsessed nameless one from among the Elohim. Wrestling heroically to win the temporal blessing of a new name, Israel—that is uniquely J's own agon.

III

Martin Noth termed the Covenant meal—what I have called a picnic on Sinai—not only the most original element of the Sinai narrative, but also noted that the silent bystanders who appear alongside of Moses in the E version seem to be competitors of Moses, since they are representatives of the host, and not of the elite. But that introduces the largest irony in the relation of J to the normative tradition. Nahum M. Sarna rightly emphasizes the Israelite innovation that marks the Sinai Covenant: there is no analogy in ancient Near Eastern history to the idea "that God and an entire people become parties to the Covenant." If my reading of J is imaginatively accurate, then J himself resisted what is central to his people's vision of itself. I think that returns one to the puzzle of J's Moses, who so clearly is not Davidic or theomorphic, unlike J's grand sequence of Abraham, Jacob, and Joseph.

Though J is, to me, no theologian, I agree with Noth's emphasis when he remarks that "the entire weight of the theology of J rests upon the beginning of his narrative." No writer, fittingly, ever has valued origins as highly as J. For him, to tell how the people were formed is to tell also what they are and what they will be. It is an oddity that J's Moses is a latecomer, while J's implied David, in Joseph, returns to the theomorphic origins. I think that accounts for why Pharaoh, in the J sequence, is so much more formidable in regard to Moses than he is in the received tradition, where he is essentially a stiff-necked despot who at last is compelled to give in. Brevard S. Childs, in his commentary on Exodus, shrewdly notes the difference in the much more imaginative J writer:

> But to J belongs the picture of Pharaoh who slyly spars with Moses, who passionately confesses his wrong, but with equal speed relents once the pressure has been removed. He can be violent (10:28) and sarcastic (10:10), almost to the extent of getting the best of the argument (10:11). He even seems to know Jewish law! Then when all is lost, the portrayal is not one of tragic despair, but of a sly fox still trying to salvage what he can (12:32).

J's Pharaoh is augmented (and entertainingly so) only because J's Moses is so deliberately less than overwhelming. If we are able to recover that scaled-down Moses, what would the consequences be, not just for how we read what we now call Exodus, but for how we regard what is now called Judaism? I take it that J keenly cared about the Yahweh of Abraham, Jacob, and Joseph (and through Joseph, of David), but that he felt a certain disinterest in the Yahweh of Moses. What if we were to emulate J? To ask such a question is not to devalue Exodus, or even to back away from Moses. What the question does involve is our freedom, as contemporary Jewish intellectuals, to return to the Yahwist's elitist concerns. Is there a way back to a vision of Yahweh that would set aside the Moses of the Priestly authors, and the Deuteronomist? *That* Moses surged on, to become the Moses of the normative sages of the Second Century of the Common Era. Is their Judaism the only authentic Judaism that ever will be available to us?

All that is constitutive of authentic Jewish belief must be the Hebrew Bible itself, but what precisely is the Bible? Genesis, Exodus, and Numbers are, for me, the J writer, and *not* the composite text in which the redactors have had the last word, a word they never earned. Unlike J, the other strands are vitiated for me not just because they are tendentious, but because their authors, unlike J, simply were not strong enough writers, not what (following Nietzsche) I would call "strong poets." To adopt Richard Rorty's post-philosophical and pragmatic formulation, they sought to achieve universality by the transcendence of J's contingency, whereas J, with Shakespeare and Homer the strongest of poets, achieved self-creation by the recognition of contingency. J created his own mind by creating his own language, whereas the redactors neither could nor would emulate J, their great original.

It is difficult to read J as J because of the deep nostalgia we feel for the normative tradition. But an awareness of J's strength gradually leads one to the realization that normative Judaism is an extremely strong misreading of the Hebrew Bible that was concluded eighteen centuries ago in order to meet the needs of the Jewish people in a Palestine under Roman occupation. Does it bind us forever as the proper version of the Covenant?

The more deeply I read in J, the more I have the same experience that I have when I read in Shakespeare, which is the revelation of radical originality. The history of J's revisionists is a long march away from J, and so becomes an endless distancing from J's Yahweh. It is a dark paradox that the Yahwist's Yahweh is not the God of normative Judaism, or of historical Christianity, or of Islam. And it is Western culture's largest irony, in our very late time, approaching the year 2000 of the Common Era, that we still need to recover the vision of God that was seen so vividly by the uncanny writer, J, who was our origin.

Moses an Egyptian

Sigmund Freud

To deny a people the man whom it praises as the greatest of its sons is not a deed to be undertaken lightheartedly—especially by one belonging to that people. No consideration, however, will move me to set aside truth in favour of supposed national interests. Moreover, the elucidation of the mere facts of the problem may be expected to deepen our insight into the situation with which they are concerned.

The man Moses, the liberator of his people, who gave them their religion and their laws, belonged to an age so remote that the preliminary question arises whether he was a historical person or a legendary figure. If he lived, his time was the thirteenth or fourteenth century B.C.; we have no word of him except from the Holy Books and the written traditions of the Jews. Although the decision lacks final historical certainty, the great majority of historians have expressed the opinion that Moses did live and that the exodus from Egypt, led by him, did in fact take place. It has been maintained with good reason that the later history of Israel could not be understood if this were not admitted. Science today has become much more cautious and deals much more leniently with tradition than it did in the early days of historical investigation.

What first attracts our interest in the person of Moses is his name, which is written Mosche in Hebrew. One may well ask: Where does it come from? What does it mean? As is well known, the story in Exodus, chapter 2, already answers this question. There we learn that the Egyptian princess who saved the babe from the waters of the Nile gave him his name, adding the etymological explanation: Because I drew him out of the water. But this explanation is obviously inadequate. "The Biblical interpretation of the name: 'He that was drawn out of the water' "—thus an author in the *Jüdisches Lexikon*—"is folk etymology; the active Hebrew form itself of the name (Mosche can at best mean only 'the drawer out') cannot be reconciled with this solution." This argument can be supported by two further reflections: first, that it is nonsensical to credit an Egyptian princess with a knowledge of Hebrew etymology, and, secondly, that the water from which the child was drawn was most probably not the water of the Nile.

On the other hand the suggestion has long been made and by many different people that the name Moses derives from the Egyptian vocabulary. Instead of citing all the authors who have voiced this opinion I shall quote a passage from a recent work by Breasted, an author whose *History of Egypt* is regarded as authoritative. "It is important to notice that his name, Moses, was Egyptian. It is simply the Egyptian word 'mose' meaning 'child,' and is an abridgement of a fuller form of such names as 'Amen-mose' meaning 'Amon-a-child' or 'Ptah-mose,' meaning 'Ptah-a-child,' these forms themselves being likewise abbreviations for the complete form 'Amon- (has-given) -a-child' or 'Ptah- (has-given) -a-child.' The abbreviation 'child' early became a convenient rapid form for the cumbrous full name, and the name Mose, 'child,' is not uncommon on the Egyptian monuments. The father of Moses without doubt prefixed to his son's name that of an Egyptian god like Amon or Ptah, and this divine name was gradually lost in current usage, till the boy was called 'Mose.' (The final *s* is an addition drawn from the Greek translation of the Old Testament. It is not in Hebrew, which has 'mosheh')." I have given this passage literally and am by no means prepared to share the responsibility for its details. I am a little surprised, however, that Breasted in citing related names should have passed over the analogous theophorous names in the list of Egyptian kings, such as Ah-mose, Thut-mose (Thotmes), and Ra-mose (Ramses).

It might have been expected that one of the many authors who recognized Moses to be an Egyptian name would have drawn the conclusion, or at least considered the possibility, that the bearer of an Egyptian name was himself an Egyptian. In modern times we have no misgiving in drawing such conclusions, although today a person bears two names, not one, and although a change of name or assimilation of it in new conditions cannot be ruled out. So we are not at all surprised to find that the poet Chamisso was of French extraction, Napoleon Buonaparte, on the other hand, of Italian, and that Benjamin Disraeli was an Italian Jew, as his name would lead us to expect. And such an inference from the name to the race should be more reliable and indeed conclusive in respect to early and primitive times. Nevertheless to the best of my knowledge no historian has drawn this conclusion in the case of Moses, not even one of those who, like Breasted, are ready to suppose that Moses "was cognizant of all the wisdom of the Egyptians."

What hindered them from doing so can only be guessed at. Perhaps the awe of biblical tradition was insuperable. Perhaps it seemed monstrous to imagine that the man Moses could have been anything other than Hebrew. In any event, what happened was that the recognition of the name being Egyptian was not a factor in judging the origin of the man Moses, and that nothing further was deduced from it. If the question of the nationality of this great man is considered important, then any new material for answering it must be welcome.

This is what my little essay attempts. The contribution it brings is an application of psychoanalysis. The considerations thus reached will impress only that minority of readers familiar with analytical reasoning and able to appreciate its conclusions. To them I hope it will appear of significance.

In 1909 Otto Rank, then still under my influence, published at my suggestion a book entitled: *Der Mythus von der Geburt des Helden*. It deals with the fact "that almost all important civilized peoples have early woven myths around and glorified in poetry their heroes, mythical kings and princes, founders of religions, of dynasties, empires and cities—in short, their national heroes. Especially the history of their birth and of their early years is furnished with phantastic traits; the amazing similarity, nay, literal identity, of those tales, even if they refer to different, completely independent peoples, sometimes geographically far removed from one another, is well known and has struck many an investigator." Following Rank we reconstruct—on the lines of Galton's technique—an "average myth" that makes prominent the essential features of all these tales, and we then get this formula:

"The hero is the son of parents of the highest station, most often the son of a king.

"His conception is impeded by difficulties, such as abstinence or temporary sterility; or else his parents practise intercourse in secret because of prohibitions or other external obstacles. During his mother's pregnancy or earlier an oracle or a dream warns the father of the child's birth as containing grave danger for his safety.

"In consequence the father (or a person representing him) gives orders for the new-born babe to be killed or exposed to extreme danger; in most cases the babe is placed in a casket and delivered to the waves.

"The child is then saved by animals or poor people, such as shepherds, and suckled by a female animal or a woman of humble birth.

"When full grown he discovers his noble parents after many strange adventures, wreaks vengeance on his father, and, recognized by his people, attains fame and greatness."

The most remote of the historical personages to whom this myth attaches is Sargon of Agade, the founder of Babylon about 2800 B.C. From the point of view of what interests us here it would perhaps be worth while to reproduce the account ascribed to himself:

"I am Sargon, the mighty king, King of Agade. My mother was a vestal; my father I knew not; while my father's brother dwelt in the mountains. In my town Azupirani—it lies on the banks of Euphrates—my mother, the vestal, conceived me. *Secretly she bore me. She laid me in a basket of sedge,* closed the opening with pitch, and *lowered me into the river.* The stream did not down me, but carried me to Akki, the drawer of water. Akki, the drawer of water, in the goodness of his heart lifted me out of the water, *Akki, the drawer of the water, as his own son he brought me up.* Akki, the drawer of water, made me his gardener. When I was a gardener, Istar fell in love with me. I became king and for forty-five years I ruled as king."

The best-known names in the series beginning with Sargon of Agade are Moses, Cyrus, and Romulus. But besides these Rank has enumerated many other heroes belonging to myth or poetry to whom the same youthful story attaches either in its entirety or in well-recognizable parts, such as Œdipus, Karna, Paris, Telephos, Perseus, Heracles, Gilgamesh, Amphion, Zethos, and others.

The source and the tendency of such myths are familiar to us through Rank's work. I need only refer to his conclusions with a few short hints. A hero is a man who stands up manfully against his father and in the end victoriously overcomes him. The myth in question traces this struggle back to the very dawn of the hero's life, by having him born against his father's will and saved in spite of his father's evil intentions. The exposure in the basket is clearly a symbolical representation of birth; the basket is the womb, the stream the water at birth. In innumerable dreams the relation of the child to the parents is represented by drawing or saving from the water. When the imagination of a people attaches this myth to a famous personage it is to indicate that he is recognized as a hero, that his life has conformed to the typical plan. The inner source of the myth is the so-called "family romance" of the child, in which the son reacts to the change in his inner relationship to his parents, especially that of his father. The child's first years are governed by grandiose over-estimation of his father; kings and queens in dreams and fairytales always represent, accordingly, the parents. Later on, under the influence of rivalry and real disappointments, the release from the parents and a critical attitude towards the father set in. The two families of the myth, the noble as well as the humble one, are therefore both images of his own family as they appear to the child in successive periods of his life.

It is not too much to say that these observations fully explain the similarity as well as the far-spread occurence of the myth of the birth of the hero. It is all the more interesting to find that the myth of Moses' birth and exposure stands apart; in one essential point it even contradicts the others.

We start with the two families between which the myth has cast the child's fate. We know that analytic interpretation makes them into one family, that the distinction is only a temporal one. In the typical form of the myth the first family, into which the child is born, is a noble and mostly a royal one; the second family, in which the child grows up, is a humble and degraded one, corresponding with the circumstances to which the interpretation refers. Only in the story of Œdipus is this difference obscured. The babe exposed by one kingly family is brought up by another royal pair. It can hardly be an accident that in this one example there is in the myth itself a glimmer of the original identity of the two families. The social contrast of the two families— meant, as we know, to stress the heroic nature of a great man—gives a second function to our myth, which becomes especially significant with historical personages. It can also be used to provide for our hero a patent of nobility to elevate him to a higher social rank. Thus Cyrus is for the Medes an alien conqueror; by way of the exposure myth he becomes the grandson of their king. A similar trait occurs in the myth of Romulus; if such a man ever lived he must have been an unknown adventurer, an upstart; the myth makes him a descendant of, and heir to, the royal house of Alba Longa.

It is very different in the case of Moses. Here the first family—usually so distinguished—is modest enough. He is the child of Jewish Levites. But the second family—the humble one in which as a rule heroes are brought up—is replaced by the royal house of Egypt; the princess brings him up as her own son. This divergence from the usual type has struck many research workers as strange. Eduard Meyer and others after him supposed the original form of the myth to have been different. Pharaoh had been warned by a prophetic dream that his daughter's son would become a danger to him and his kingdom. This is why he has the child delivered to the waters of the Nile shortly after his birth. But the child is saved by Jewish people and brought up as their own. "National motives," in Rank's terminology, had transformed the myth into the form now known by us.

However, further thought tells us that an original Moses myth of this kind, one not diverging from other birth myths, could not have existed. For the legend is either of Egyptian or of Jewish origin. The first supposition may be excluded. The Egyptians had no motive to glorify Moses; to them he was not a hero. So the legend should have originated among the Jewish people; that is to say, it was attached in the usual version to the person of their leader. But for that purpose it was entirely unfitted; what good is a legend to a people that makes their hero into an alien?

The Moses myth as we know it today lags sadly behind its secret motives. If Moses is not of royal lineage our legend cannot make him into a hero; if he remains a Jew it has done nothing to raise his status. Only one small feature of the whole myth remains effective: the assurance that the babe survived in spite of strong outside forces to the contrary. This feature is repeated in the early history of Jesus, where King Herod assumes the role of Pharoah. So we really have a right to assume that in a later and rather clumsy treatment of the legendary material the adapter saw fit to equip his hero Moses with certain features appertaining to the classical exposure myths characteristic of a hero, and yet unsuited to Moses by reason of the special circumstances.

With this unsatisfactory and even uncertain result our investigation would have to end, without having contributed anything to answering the question whether Moses was Egyptian, were there not another and perhaps more successful way of approaching the exposure myth itself.

Let us return to the two families of the myth. As we know, on the level of analytic interpretation they are identical. On a mythical level they are distinguished as the noble and the humble family. With a historical person to whom the myth has become attached there is, however, a third level, that of reality. One of the families is the real one, the one into which the great man was really born and in which he was brought up. The other is fictitious, invented by the myth in pursuance of its own motives. As a rule the real family corresponds with the humble one, the noble family with the fictitious one. In the case of Moses something seemed to be different. And here the new point of view may perhaps bring some illumination. It is that the first family, the one from which the babe is exposed to danger, is in all comparable cases the fictitious one; the second family, however, by which the hero is adopted and in which he grows up, is his real one. If we have the courage to accept this statement as a general truth to which the Moses legend also is subject, then we suddenly see our way clear. Moses is an Egyptian—probably of noble origin—whom the myth undertakes to transform into a Jew. And that would be our conclusion! The exposure in the water was in its right place; to fit the new conclusion the intention had to be changed, not without violence. From a means of getting rid of the child it becomes a means of its salvation.

The divergence of the Moses legend from all others of its kind might be traced back to a special feature in the story of Moses' life. Whereas in all other cases the hero rises above his humble beginnings as his life progresses, the heroic life of the man Moses began by descending from his eminence to the level of the children of Israel.

This little investigation was undertaken in the hope of gaining from it a second, fresh argument for the suggestion that Moses was an Egyptian. We have seen that the first argument, that of his name, has not been considered decisive. We have to be prepared for the new reasoning—the analysis of the exposure myth—not faring any better. The objection is likely to be that the circumstances of the origin and transformation of legends are too obscure to allow of such a conclusion as the preceding one, and that all efforts to extract the kernel of historical truth must be doomed to failure in face of the incoherence and contradictions clustering around the heroic person of Moses and the unmistakable signs of tendentious distortion and stratification accumulated through many centuries. I myself do not share this negative attitude, but I am not in a position to confute it.

If there was no more certainty than this to be attained, why have I brought this inquiry to the notice of a wider public? I regret that even my justification has to restrict itself to hints. If, however, one is

attracted by the two arguments outlined above and tries to take seriously the conclusion that Moses was a distinguished Egyptian, then
very interesting and far-reaching perspectives open out. With the help
of certain assumptions the motives guiding Moses in his unusual
undertaking can be made intelligible; in close connection with this the
possible motivation of numerous characteristics and peculiarities of the
legislation and religion he gave the Jewish people can be perceived. It
stimulates ideas of some moment concerning the origin of monotheistic religion in general. But such important considerations cannot be
based on psychological probabilities alone. Even if one were to accept it
as historical that Moses was Egyptian, we should want at least one
other fixed point so as to protect the many emerging possibilities from
the reproach of their being products of imagination and too far removed from reality. An objective proof of the period into which the
life of Moses, and with it the exodus from Egypt, fall would perhaps
have sufficed. But this has not been forthcoming, and therefore it will
be better to suppress any inferences that might follow our view that
Moses was an Egyptian. . . .

If, then, Moses was an Egyptian, the first gain from this suggestion is a new riddle, one difficult to answer. When a people of a tribe
prepares for a great undertaking, it is to be expected that one of them
should make himself their leader or be chosen for this role. But what
could have induced a distinguished Egyptian—perhaps a prince, priest,
or high official—to place himself at the head of a throng of culturally
inferior immigrants, and to leave the country with them, is not easy to
conjecture. The well-known contempt of the Egyptians for foreigners
makes such a proceeding especially unlikely. Indeed, I am inclined to
think this is why even those historians who recognized the name as
Egyptian, and ascribed all the wisdom of Egypt to him, were not
willing to entertain the obvious possibility that Moses was an Egyptian.
    This first difficulty is followed by a second. We must not forget
that Moses was not only the political leader of the Jews settled in
Egypt; he was also their lawgiver and educator and the man who
forced them to adopt a new religion, which is still today called Mosaic
after him. But can a single person create a new religion so easily? And
when someone wishes to influence the religion of another, would not
the most natural thing be to convert him to his own? The Jewish
people in Egypt were certainly not without some kind of religion, and

if Moses, who gave them a new religion, was an Egyptian, then the surmise cannot be rejected that this other new religion was the Egyptian one.

This possibility encounters an obstacle: the sharp contrast between the Jewish religion attributed to Moses and the Egyptian one. The former is a grandiosely rigid monotheism. There is only one God, unique, omnipotent, unapproachable. The sight of his countenance cannot be borne; one must not make an image of him, nor even breathe his name. In the Egyptian religion, on the other hand, there is a bewildering mass of deities of differing importance and provenance. Some of them are personifications of great natural powers like heaven and earth, sun and moon. Then we find an abstraction such as Maat (Justice, Truth) or a grotesque creature like the dwarfish Bes. Most of them, however, are local gods from the time when the land was divided into numerous provinces. They have the shapes of animals as if they had not yet overcome their origin in the old totem animals. They are not clearly differentiated, barely distinguished by special functions attributed to some of them. The hymns in praise of these gods tell the same thing about each of them, identify them with one another without any misgivings, in a way that would confuse us hopelessly. Names of deities are combined with one another, so that one becomes degraded almost to an epithet of the other. Thus in the best period of the "New Empire" the main god of the city of Thebes is called Amon-Re, in which combination the first part signifies the ram-headed city-god, whereas Re is the name of the hawk-headed sun-god of On. Magic and ceremonial, amulets and formulas dominated the service of these gods, as they did the daily life of the Egyptians.

Some of these differences may easily derive from the contrast in principle between a strict monotheism and an unlimited polytheism. Others are obviously consequences of a difference in intellectual level; one religion is very near to the primitive, the other has soared to the heights of sublime abstraction. Perhaps it is these two characteristics that occasionally give one the impression that the contrast between the Mosaic and the Egyptian religion is one intended and purposely accentuated; for example, when the one religion severely condemns any kind of magic or sorcery, which flourishes so abundantly in the other; or when the insatiable zest of the Egyptian for making images of his gods in clay, stone, and metal, to which our museums owe so much, is contrasted with the way in which the making of the image of any living or visionary being is bluntly forbidden.

There is yet another difference between the two religions which the explanations I have attempted do not touch. No other people of antiquity has done so much to deny death, has made such careful provision for an after-life; in accordance with this the death-god Osiris, the ruler of that other world, was the most popular and indisputable of all Egyptian gods. The early Jewish religion, on the other hand, had entirely relinquished immortality; the possibility of an existence after death was never mentioned in any place. And this is all the more remarkable since later experience has shown that the belief in a life beyond can very well be reconciled with a monotheistic religion.

I had hoped the suggestion that Moses was an Egyptian would prove enlightening and stimulating in many different respects. But our first deduction from this suggestion—that the new religion he gave the Jews was his own, the Egyptian one—has foundered on the difference—nay, the striking contrast—between the two religions.

The Burning Bush (Exodus 3)

Martin Buber

The section that deals with the Revelation at the Burning Bush (Exod. 3:1–4, 17) cannot be regarded as a compilation from varying sources and documents. All that is needed is to remove a few additions, and there appears before us a homogeneous picture; any apparent contradiction can be accounted for by the fact that the text has not been fully understood. The style and composition of this section show that it is the fruit of a highly cultivated dialectic and narrative art; but certain of the essential elements of which it is composed bear the stamp of early tradition.

Moses, tending the flocks of his father-in-law, leads them out of the accustomed steppe on one occasion: just as we hear of the Bedouins of the same district moving with their flocks into the hills, where the animals find pastures that are still green. There Moses suddenly finds himself at the "Mountain of God," Mount Horeb or Sinai. "Mountain of God" (or "of gods") had been its name since time untold, presumably because mysterious phenomena, either of volcanic or other character, take place on it and local tradition therefore claims that divine beings reside there. Here Moses sees the "burning bush." Just as the mountain is described as "*the* mountain of God," that is, the mountain known as "a god-mountain" (only after the revelation to the people in Numbers 10:33 is it called "the Mountain of YHVH"), so is the bush described as "*the* thornbush," that is, the specific bush that is known to grow upon Sinai. The name *seneh* which is peculiar to it (no other kind of bush is called so) echoes the name of the mountain, which is omitted of set purpose at this point. The word *seneh* repeated three times in the

From *On the Bible: Eighteen Studies by Martin Buber.* © 1968 by Schocken Books, Inc.

same sentence suggests the name Sinai, which is used only (16:1) when the nation reaches the mountain in order to receive the revelation.

The bush burns, the blaze flares up, and in the blaze the "messenger of YHVH" is seen by Moses. Such "messengers" (which we call "angels") are always recorded in the earlier Scriptures without personal names, and, so to say, without personal character. They are nothing save the perceptible intervention of God in events, which is sometimes made even more plain by the fact that they and YHVH Himself are alternately named as speakers.

The flame does not consume the bush. This is not a consuming fire that nourishes itself on the material it has seized, and is itself extinguished in the destruction of that material. The bush blazes but is not consumed: and in the blaze shining forth from it, Moses sees the "messenger."

Certain scholars take the story to mean that "on Sinai there was a holy thornbush which was considered by the residents of the region to be the seat of the mountain divinity," and they draw the conclusion that YHVH "is also regarded here as a tree god." They find support from the fact that in the "Blessing of Moses" (Deut. 33:16) the god is designated *shokhni seneh,* which is translated as "He who dwells in the thornbush." The verb in question, however, did not originally mean to dwell but to take up residence; to sojourn, no matter how temporarily. Further, the apparition is not seen in the plant but in the fire; and accordingly the voice that calls Moses "from the midst of the bush" (Exod. 3:4) should be understood as coming from the fire which blazes throughout the entire bush. YHVH, to be sure, can just as little be regarded here as mountain god—He who attacks Moses on the way to Egypt (4:24) and orders Aaron in Egypt (4:27); and in our story He already states the deeds He would perform there in support of Moses. All these are characteristics the like of which are not reported of any of the mountain gods, and which (apart from the fact that YHVH Himself says [3:8] that He has "come down" from heaven) speak against the view that Moses had "discovered the seat of YHVH."

There are some who tend to "draw a distinction in principle" between the calling of Moses, which commenced with this apparition, and the calling of the prophets; "for whereas the latter undergo a psychological experience which takes place in dream or vision, there is a mythical event in the case of Moses, since the Divinity appears to him corporeally." This is a distinction in categories which finds nothing in the Bible text to support it. Isaiah says (Isa. 6:5), apparently in a memorial written many years after the event reported, that his eyes had seen "the King YHVH of Hosts"; which is not less but rather more corporeal than the apparition described in the story of the summoning of Moses. For it is made perfectly clear here that Moses saw no form. After the messenger permitted himself to be seen "in the blazing fire," what Moses sees is expressly stated: "and there, the bush was burning with fire, but the bush was not consumed." That it was this he saw and nothing else is also stressed by the fact that he says to himself: "Let me go across, and see this great sight—why the thornbush is not burnt up." Nobody who had seen a divine form in the fire could talk in that way. Moses actually sees the messenger *in* the blaze; he sees nothing other than this. When he sees the wondrous fire he sees what he has to see. No matter how we explain the process as being natural, this at least is what the narrative tells us and wishes to tell us; and whatever this may be, it is clearly not "mythology."

As against this the difference between the literary categories of saga and prophecy is indicated in scholarly quarters, and the explanation is given that literary history must "*ab initio* protest at the obliteration of the saga-like character"; no scientific investigator, it is claimed, would even dare "to derive the legends of Hellenic heroes, whose eyes so often saw divinities, from psychological experiences." Yet with all the deference to literary categories, their scientific dignity is not great enough to decide the character and dimension of the content of truth in an account of a revelation; it is not even enough to ensure the correct formulation of the question. Instead of the legends of Greek heroes let those of Greek thinkers be taken—say that of Pythagoras, which appears to have influenced the late Alexandrian version of Moses' life story—and it will immediately be seen that we are to face to face with the problem of a transmitted nucleus of personal experience contained in it—naturally without even thinking of being able to extract that nucleus. How much more so when it comes to a vision so singular, so characteristic, despite certain external analogies, as that of the Burning Bush, followed by such a conversation as the one that follows. It compels us to forsake the pale of literature for that singular region where great personal religious experiences are propagated in ways that can no longer be identified.

YHVH sees Moses approach to look; and "God" (here of set purpose not "YHVH" appears as the acting one, as previously, but "God"), in order to establish the connection with the "messenger," calls to Moses from out of the bush. It has correctly been remarked that such a calling

by God from a specific place occurs only three times in the story of
Moses, and that each of them is made from a different one of the three
sites of revelation: once, in our text, from the bush, once (Exod. 19:3)
from the mountain, and once (Lev. 1:1) at the Tent of Meeting. The
biblical work of redaction indeed shows wisdom and art of a rare kind.
The passage now under consideration differs from the others by the
fact that Moses is called on by name. That is the fashion in which
divinity establishes contact with one chosen. The latter, not conscious
yet aware of the One whose voice is calling him, places himself at the
service of the God by his words "here I am"; and the God first orders
him not to come closer (the restriction on the "approach" to the
Divinity is one of the basic provisions of biblical religion) and to
remove the sandals from his feet. The reason may possibly be because,
being holy ground, it should not be trodden by any occupying and
therefore possessing shoe (cf. Ruth 4:7). It is only now that God tells
him who He is; He who communicates with him, Moses, here in
strange parts, is none other than the god of his forefathers, the God of
the Fathers; and hence, as we may suppose, the God of whom Moses
must have heard yonder in Egypt when he went forth every day "unto
his brethen."

The favored "Kenite" hypothesis explains that YHVH was unknown to Israel until then, being a mountain, a fire, or maybe a
volcanic god and simultaneously the tribal god of the Kenites (who are
often assumed to have been wandering smiths) and that Moses had
"discovered" this god at His seat of worship on Sinai. This hypothesis
is unfounded. There are not the faintest indications that any god of the
name was ever honored in that district. No more than suppositions are
possible with regard to the character and qualities of a, or the, putative
Kenite god. For this reason the hypothesis has not unjustly been
described as "an explanation of *ignotum ab ignoto.*" We know of YHVH's
connection with Sinai only from the Bible; and what we know is that
at the time of the exodus of the Children of Israel from Egypt YHVH
had selected Sinai as the seat for His manifestation. The Song of
Deborah, which is referred to (Judg. 5:5), does not bring YHVH, as is
supposed, from Sinai to the Galilean battlefield; it only ascribes the
name "a Sinai" to Mount Tabor, from which (4:6) the God who had
come in storm clouds out of the south revealed Himself in the glorious
victory over His foes. And Elijah, who is thought to have made a
pilgrimage to Sinai when he wished to "speak personally to and seek
an audience of YHVH," really wandered defeated and weary of life to

the mountain in order to lay himself down and perish in "the cave" (1 Kings 19:9), that is, in yonder cleft in the rock (Exod. 33:22), familiar to the wanderers, from which Moses had once seen the God passing by. YHVH never appears in the tales of His revelations to Moses and Israel as "fixed" on Sinai; He only comes down thither on occasion, decending from heaven to do so (Exod. 3:8; 19:18, 20). Comparative religion, too, is familiar with mountains not merely as the divine seat, but also as the place where gods manifest themselves.

And just as this does not make Him a mountain god, so the fact that in the course of the revelation He often makes use of the element of fire, the heavenly origin of which is frequently referred to in the Bible, does not convert Him into a fire god. For our purpose, however, the most important fact is not the traits of the nature gods that He has absorbed (criticism of these particular characteristics is offered in the story of the Sinai revelation to Elijah; cf. 1 Kings 19:11f.) but what He is to begin with. Is He an alien god whom Moses meets, and through Moses, Israel, and who is made the national god of Israel by Moses? Or is He a "God of the Fathers"?

The Bible permits us to ascertain this. All we have to do is to compare the peculiarities of the God of Moses with those of the God of the Fathers. More precisely, it is our concern to reveal the peculiar divine likeness, first in the constituents of our tale which, beyond all question, lead back to early tradition, and then in the corresponding elements of the other, a likeness, that is to say, that it is impossible simply to classify by some type or other of the pre-Mosaic religious history of the Ancient East, for despite all its relationships with one or another of these types, it shows a character differing from them all. Thereafter we must compare the two divine likenesses with one another.

If the material in the Bible is subjected to such an examination, the two likenesses will be found to differ in a special manner; namely, just as a clan god in non-historical situations might be expected to differ from a national god in a historical situation. Yet at the same time it can be observed that both depict the identical god. To begin with the former, the clan god: we immediately observe two main characteristics which are both demonstrated in his relation to the men chosen by him. One is that he approaches these men, addresses them, manifests himself to them, demands and charges them and accepts them in his covenant; and the second, closely connected with the first, that he does not remain satisfied with withdrawing them from their surrounding world and sending them on new paths, but wanders with them himself and guides them along those new paths; meanwhile, however, remaining invisible insofar as he does not "make himself seen" by them. Taken both together, these cannot be compared with the attributes of any other divinity in the history of religion, despite certain analogies of detail. The prerequisite assumption for both is that this god is not bound to any place, and that the seats of his manifestations do not restrict him; above them open the gates of heaven (Gen. 28:17), through which he descends and returns to his inaccessible realm.

We find all this once more in the second likeness, in the national god; but here it has the vivid color of a historical driving force. The new and supplementary characteristics, striking as they may appear, nevertheless seem peripheral to us when compared with the central power of the common element. Once again the God makes His great demands of His men, commanding and promising, establishing a covenant with them. But now He no longer turns to single persons but to a people, and that people too He leads forth and Himself conducts along the new way. Once again the invisible One becomes manifest from time to time. Once again heaven and earth are joined, and the God utters His words from heaven unto earth (Exod. 20:22).

This is no alien god "discovered" by Moses on Sinai; it is the God of the Fathers. And yet it is in his eyes none other than the God of whom his wife's kinsfolk may have told him, saying that He dwells on this mountain. When Moses came to the Midianites, he entered the range of life of the Fathers; and he senses the apparition he now sees as being that of the God of the Fathers. As YHVH had once gone down with Jacob to Egypt (Gen. 46:4), so has He now gone from Egypt to Midian; possibly with Moses himself, who was obviously under His protection like Jacob of old. At all events Moses perceives who it is that appears to him; he recognizes Him. That was what had happened in the days of the Fathers too. Abraham had recognized YHVH in the El 'Elyon of Melchizedek, YHVH had permitted himself to be seen (16:7, 13) by Abraham's concubine, the Egyptian maid Hagar, as the spirit of a desert spring—seemingly one of those divinatory springs at which something can be "seen" during sleep. What happens here, as it had happened there, is, from the point of view of religious history, an identification. The God brought with and accompanying a man is identified with the one known as previously to be found at this spot; He becomes recognized in him. From Babylonian and Egyptian religious thought we know the tendency to give full expression to the faith in the supremacy of a single god by interpreting the other gods as his forms of manifestation. But with the exception of the short-lived imperialistic theology of Amenhotep IV, no serious attempt in this direction was or could be made in the great pantheons. Only in the religious atmosphere of a solitary exclusive God outside the pantheons, claiming and leading His own men, could any such identification become a living reality.

Attention deserves to be given to the fact that YHVH addresses Moses not merely as the God of the Fathers, but first as the God of his (i.e., Moses' own) father. Later on this was, at times, no longer understood, as can be seen in the text of the Samaritans which knows only a "God of thy fathers." But the biblical narrative lets Moses (Exod. 18:4) say when naming a son: "the God of my father was my aid." Only Jacob before him in the Bible spoke of himself both personally and yet in relation to past generations (Gen. 31:5, 42; 32:10). Nobody spoke in that way after him. Here too can be felt the peculiar relation with the world of the patriarchs. And, whatever may be the position in disentangling the sources, the redactor knew well what he was doing when he introduced those passages, in which the man who had grown up in his own father's home is shown to be conscious of his God as the God of his own father.

After the God tells His chosen one who He is, He reveals the cause and purpose of the message with which He wishes to entrust him. The sentence with which this partial address begins and that with which it ends balance one another like the members of a building, through the two key words *ammi*, my people, and *Mitzraim*, Egypt. These are repeated in both, and denote the subject and the aim of the act: "I have indeed seen the sufferings of my people who are in Egypt," and "lead out my people the children of Israel from Egypt." To attribute the two sentences, as is so often done, to different sources constitutes a misunderstanding of the entire form and sense of the speech. With this repeated "my people" at the commencement and close of the passage, YHVH recognizes Israel in a fashion more powerful and unequivocal than would have been possible by any other verbal means. To be sure, He has not yet designated Himself their God. He will become the God of Israel as a people solely through the revelation to the people; now He wishes to be known only as the God of their forefathers, to whom He had once promised the land whither He would lead Israel. But since He so stresses the naming of Israel as His people, He shows that the bond uniting them had been established of old. No new, no alien god talks in such a way. This likewise indicates the hopelessness of the attempt sometimes made to attribute this first speech, which refers to the patriarchs, to some later stratum of the text. Try to insert at this point the phrase assumed to have been in the original, namely "I am the god," i.e., "I am the god of this mountain," and the message, flaming with historical revelation and historical faith, shrinks, one might well say, to a private remark that conveys nothing.

And now begins the great duologue in which the God commands and the man resists. As we have it before us, it is clearly disfigured by supplements, inserted by editors, which should not be considered as sections of a sourse. To begin with, something is introduced between the two first objections of the resisting man, namely his inadequacy and his inability to tell the people what they would demand to hear of the name and hence of the character of the God, on the one hand; and the final passage which returns once again to his inadequacy, on the other. In the interpolated passage Moses asks how he can demonstrate the reliability of his message to the people and is instructed to perform wonders. Here later narrative motifs are introduced in evidence, largely in order to link the story of the revelation with that of the negotiations with Pharaoh; but by this both sections are impaired. The style differs here from that in the undoubtedly genuine parts of the narrative of the Burning Bush; it is more loose, more expansive, more wordy. Here necessity does not hold sway as it does there; the purposeful repetitions are replaced by casual ones; and finally a rhetorical note is to be heard. The hard rhythm has become a thin absence of rhythm, the firm composition has become negligent; even the structure of the sentences is careless. The contents do not resemble those of the genuine parts; questions and answers move at a lower level. In the genuine part every reply gives some essential information as to the will and work of the God; but here there is, so to speak, a technical atmosphere. The clearest sign of the difference, however, is that the word "sign" is used here in a sense differing entirely from the one in which it is used there. In the genuine parts it is used in accordance with prophetic terminology. (For instance, compare Isa. 20:3, where the prophet's nakedness appears as a sign, or Ezek. 4:3, where the erection of an iron wall which separates the prophet from the city of Jerusalem has the same function.) It is a symbolization, a sensory presentation of a manifested truth, a perceptible reality which, no matter whether it is more or less "wondrous," always reminds people once again of that truth. In the same sense, after Moses says (Exod. 3:11): "Who am I that I should go

to Pharaoh and that I should lead the children of Israel out of Egypt?"
YHVH provides the assurance "Indeed I shall be present with you," and
He promises Moses a "sign" which at first seems strange to us: that the
people would come to this same mountain, where they would engage
in the service of their God; and this is what must serve Moses as a sign
that it is this same God who has sent him. We have to understand this
as meaning: what is now only existent in words will then take on real
existence. Then Moses will experience the mission of this God as an
expression of His being; not as a spiritual mission, as now, but as a
reality apparent to the senses. Unlike this, the word "sign" in the
supplement (4:8f.) appears as a proof of reliability produced by way of
supernatural arts, which have no inner relationship with the truth
intended; a meaning that is alien to the prophetic sphere. (The case of
Isa. 8:8, 11, for example, is not concerned with a proof; the "sign"
proposed there is not a proof.)

If we omit this supplement, however, together with the seven
final verses of chapter 3, all written in a later and rhetorical style
(reminiscent of the late parts of Deuteronomy), which were also clearly
introduced in order to link the passage with the following events, we
are left with a narrative religious document of almost incomparable
purity, in which every word is evidence of its derivation from the
hands of an early prophet, who worked up elements offered to him by
tradition in the light of his own basic experience. The resistance
offered to the mission, which was opposed to all the natural tendencies
of the one charged, and the breaking down of this resistance by the
divine power, belong, as shown us by the autobiographical notes of
Jeremiah and the paradigmatic little book on Jonah (the nucleus of
which may derive from the eighth century B.C.), to the most intimate
experience of the prophetic man.

The first objection, that of his own smallness compared with the
vast task, corresponds precisely, after eliminating the supplements, to
the third (4:10), in which Moses stresses his difficulty of speech. And
once again, after YHVH responds that He, the God of Creation, makes
the mouth of man to speak or be dumb, and therefore made Moses
himself as he is, and sends him just as he is, YHVH continues: "Go, I
myself shall be present with your mouth and shall instruct you what
you should say." Here ends the original wording of the narrative.
(Verses 13–16, repeating the motif "I shall be present with you" once
again, but without inner necessity, are formed on a variant to 7:1, and
have clearly been inserted in order to introduce Moses' brother Aaron,

"the Levite," the forefather of the priesthood, at this early point, as fellow carrier of the divine will. This complement actually has a later stamp than the original tale, but an earlier one than the supplements. Verse 17 derives from the author of the second supplement.)

It is necessary to bear in mind the two promises of the speaking God that begin with the word *ehyeh,* "I shall be," I shall be present, assuring that He would remain present amid His chosen, in order properly to understand the central part of the duologue, the central question and the central response, framed by these two pillars.

The point at issue here is not Man but God, the name of God. The words of Moses are generally taken to mean that he wished to learn the answer he would have to give the people if they asked him to tell them the name of the God whose message he brought. Understood in this sense, the passage becomes one of the chief supports of the Kenite hypothesis, since it is scarcely possible to imagine that any people would not know the name of the God of their fathers. If you wish to ask a person's name in biblical Hebrew, however, you never say, as is done here, "What (*mah*) is his name?" or "What is your name?" but "Who (*mi*) are you?" "Who is he?" "Who (*mi*) is your name?" "Tell me your name." Where the word "what" is associated with the word "name," the question asked is what finds expression in or lies concealed behind that name.

When the "man" with whom Jacob wrestled at the ford of Jabbok asks him "What is your name?" (Gen. 32:28), the point at issue is that this name can be given the reproach of an interpretation as "heel-sneak" (cf. Gen. 27:36 and Hos. 12:4). Now, however, the new name Israel is intended to take away the reproach of the old: "Not Jacob, Heel-sneak, should any longer be uttered as your name." That is the change which is to be introduced through the mention of the old name by the one who bears it. In simpler form, and without dialogue, this takes place again when God fulfills the promise (Gen. 35:10).

The phrase "What is His name?" appears once more in a gnomic saying (Prov. 30:4); but here the question asked is certainly not the name of the One who "has established all the ends of the earth." The speaker is presumably well aware of that; the subject of the question is not sound but mystery. Moses expects the people to ask the meaning and character of a name of which they have been aware since the days of their fathers. Which name? From the answer of the God it can be seen that the question refers to YHVH.

In a later manifestation (Exod. 6:3), YHVH informs Moses that He was seen by the forefathers "in El Shaddai," that is, in the quality of a Shaddai God; but "by my name YHVH I did not make myself known to them." What Shaddai is can only be guessed from the word and the circumstances under which it is used in the stories of the patriarchs; yet the name clearly means the Divinity as Power; and, as seems to be indicated by five of the six passages in Genesis where the name is found, as the power making the human clan fruitful. Therefore the term can be taken to imply the power founding the tribe. Here, indeed, the issue is the biological development of Israel, which is understood as a divine work. The name YHVH, it is true, is introduced only once in the Genesis narrative in the form of a direct revelatory speech placed in the mouth of the God (Gen. 15:7), and in the identical form of phrase with which the revelation to the people begins (Exod. 20:2). But Abraham proclaims the name when he comes to Canaan as might a herald, at one spot after another (which should not be understood as a calling in prayer), and his clan knows the name. Is it likely that the author of Exodus 6:3 did not know this? Here, however, what is said is not that the patriarchs made no use of the name of YHVH, but only that they did not know him in the quality characterized by this name; and that this had now been discovered. What can that mean?

Of all the various suppositions regarding the prehistoric use of the name YHVH there is only one the development of which makes all this understandable without contradiction. To the best of my knowledge it was first expressed nearly half a century ago by Bernhard Duhm in an (unpublished) lecture at Göttingen: "Possibly the name is in some degree only an extension of the word *hu,* meaning he, as God is also called by other Arab tribes at times of religious revival—the One, the Unnamable." The Dervish cry *ya-hu* is interpreted to mean. "O He!" and in one of the most important poems of the Persian mystic Jelaluddin Rumi, the following occurs: "One I seek, One I know, One I see, One I call. He is the first, He is the last, He is the outward, He is the inward. I know no other except *Yahu* (O He) and *Ya-man-hu* (O-He-who-is)." The original form of the cry may have been *Ya-huva,* if we regard the Arabic pronoun *huwa,* he, as the original Semitic form of the pronoun "he" which, in Hebrew as well as in another Arabic form, has become *hu.* "The name *Ya-huva* would then mean O-He! with which the manifestations of the god would be greeted in the cult when the god became perceptible in some fashion. Such a *Ya-huva* could afterwards produce both *Yahu* and Yahveh (possibly originally *Yahvah*)." Similar divine names deriving from "primitive sounds" are also known in other religions, but in, say, the Dionysos cult the cries developed into corresponding nouns, whereas the Semites preserved the elemental cry itself as a name. Such a name, which has an entirely oral character and really requires completion by some such gesture as, for example, the throwing out of an arm, is, to be sure (as long, at least, as the undertone of the third person still affects the consciousness of speaker and listener) more suitable for evocation than for invocation. As an invocation it appears in the story of the patriarchs only in a cry (Gen. 49:18) which strangely interrupts the continuity of the blessings of Jacob. This may also explain why during the pre-Mosaic period scarcely any personal names are recorded as having been formed with this divine name. The only known exception, as it would appear, is the name of Moses' mother, Yochebed, which apparently means "YHVH is weighty." If so, it might possibly be regarded as a sign of some specific family tradition, which prepares the way for a new relation to the divine name.

Certainly it is more typical that in the course of the ages, particularly at an epoch of increasing religious laxity, as the Egyptian period appears to have been for Israel, the element of excitation and discharge connected with the calling of the name did not merely ebb away, but the name itself degenerated into a sound simultaneously empty and half forgotten. Under such conditions an hour might well come when the people would ask this question of a man bringing them a message from the God of their fathers: "How about His name?" That means: "What is this God really like? We cannot find out from His name!" For as far as primitive human beings are concerned, the name of a person indicates his character.

But there is also something else included in the question, namely the expression of a negative experience that the enslaved people had had with this God of theirs: "After all, He never troubled about us all this while! When the Egyptians require their gods, they invoke them by uttering their 'true' names in the correct fashion, and the gods come and do what is necessary. But we have not been able to invoke Him, we cannot invoke Him. How can we be certain of Him, how can we bring Him into our power? How can we make use of His name? What about His name?"

The "true" name of a person, like that of any other object, is far more than a mere denotative designation, for men who think in categories of magic; it is the essence of the person, distilled from his real being, so that he is present in it once again. What is more, he is present in it in such a form that anybody who knows the true name and knows how to pronounce it in the correct way can gain control of him. The person himself is unapproachable, he offers resistance; but through the name he becomes approachable, the speaker has power over him. The true name may be entirely different from the generally familiar one that covers it; it may also, however, differ from the latter only in the "correct" pronunciation, which would also include the correct rhythm and the correct attitude of the body while engaged in the act of pronouncing it; all things that can only be taught and transmitted personally. And since the true name phoneticizes the character of the object, the essential thing in the last resort is that the speaker shall recognize this essential being in the name, and direct his full attention upon it. Where that happens, where the magical work requires an aiming of the soul at the being meant, that is, when the "person" aimed at is a god or a demon, the fuel is provided into which the lightning of a religious experience can fall. Then the magical compulsion becomes the intimacy of prayer, the bundle of utilizable forces bearing a personal name becomes a Thou, and a demagization of existence takes place.

As reply to his question about the name, Moses is told: *Ehyeh asher ehyeh.* This is usually understood to mean "I am that I am" in the sense that YHVH describes Himself as the Being One or even the Everlasting One, the one unalterably persisting in His being. But that would be abstraction of a kind that does not usually come about in periods of increasing religious vitality; while in addition the verb in the biblical language does not carry this particular shade of meaning of pure existence. It means: happening, coming into being, being there, being present, being thus and thus; but not being in an abstract sense. "I am that I am" could only be understood as an avoiding of the question, as a "statement which withholds any information." Should we, however, really assume that in the view of the narrator the God who came to inform His people of their liberation wishes, at that hour of all hours, merely to secure His distance, and not to grant and warrant proximity as well? This concept is certainly discouraged by that twofold *ehyeh,* "I shall be present" (Exod. 3:12; 4:12), which precedes and follows the statement with unmistakable intention, and in which God promises to be present with those chosen by Him, to remain present with them, to assist them. This promise is given unconditional validity in the first part of the statement: "I shall be present," not merely, as previously and subsequently, "with you, with your mouth," but absolutely, "I shall be present." Placed as the phrase is between two utterances of so concrete a kind, that clearly means: I am and remain present. Behind it stands the implied reply to those influenced by the magical practices of Egypt, those infected by technical magic: it is superfluous for you to wish to invoke me; in accordance with my character I again and again stand by those whom I befriend; and I would have you know indeed that I befriend you.

This is followed in the second part by: "That I shall be present," or "As which I shall be present." In this way the sentence is reminiscent of the later statement of the God to Moses: "I shall be merciful to him to whom I shall be merciful" (33:19). But in it the future character is more strongly stressed. YHVH indeed states that He will always be present, but at any given moment as the one as whom He then, in that given moment, will be present. He who promises His steady presence, His steady assistance, refuses to restrict Himself to definite forms of manifestation; how could the people even venture to conjure and limit Him! If the first part of the statement says: "I do not need to be conjured for I am always with you," the second adds: "but it is impossible to conjure me."

It is necessary to remember Egypt as the background of such a revelation: Egypt where the magician went so far as to threaten the gods that if they would not do his will he would not merely betray their names to the demons, but would also tear the hair from their heads as lotus blossoms are pulled out of the pond. Here religion was in practice little more than regulated magic. In the revelation at the Burning Bush religion is demagicized.

At the same time, however, the meaning and character of the divine name itself changes; that is, from the viewpoint of the narrator as well as from that of the tradition given shape by him, it is unfolded in its true sense. By means of the introduction of an inconsiderable change in vocalization, a change to which the consciousness of sound would not be too sensitive, a wildly ecstatic outcry, half interjection half pronoun, is replaced by a grammatically precise verbal form which, in the third person (*havah* is the same as *hayh*—to be—but belongs to an older stratum of language), means the same as is communicated by the *ehyeh:* YHVH is "He who will be present" or "He who is here," He who is present here; not merely some time and some where but in every now and in every here. Now the name expresses His character and assures the faithful of the richly protective presence of their Lord.

And it is the God Himself who unfolds His name after this fashion. The exclamation was its hidden form; the verb is its revelation. And in order to make it clear beyond all possibility of misapprehension that the direct word *ehyeh* explains the indirect name, Moses is first instructed, by an exceptionally daring linguistic device, to tell the people "*Ehyeh,* I shall be present, or I am present, sends me to you," and immediately afterwards: "YHVH the God of your fathers sends me to you." That *ehyeh* is not a name; the God can never be named so; only on this one occasion, in this sole moment of transmitting His work, is Moses allowed and ordered to take the God's self-comprehension in his mouth as a name. But when, shortly before the destruction of the Northern Kingdom of Israel, the prophet Hosea, in order to give concrete expression to the impending crisis in national history, calls his newborn son *Lo-ammi,* not my people, he justifies this name with the divine word: "you are not my people and I am not *ehyeh* for you" (Hos. 1:9). One expects to hear: ". . . and I am not your God," but what is said is: "For you I am no longer *ehyeh,* that is, 'I am present.' " The unfaithful people lose the presence of their God, the name revealed is concealed from them once again. Just as the *Lo-ammi* refers to the *ammi* of the Burning Bush episode, so does this *ehyeh* refer to that.

Again and again, when God says in the narrative: "Then will the Egyptians recognize that I am YHVH," or "you will recognize that I am YHVH," it is clearly not the name as a sound, but the meaning revealed in it that is meant. The Egyptians shall come to know that I (unlike their gods) am the really present One in the midst of the human world, the standing and acting One; you will know that I am He who is present with you, going with you and directing your cause. And until the very close of the Babylonian Exile, and later, sayings such as "I am YHVH, that is my name" (Isa. 42:8), or even more clearly, "Therefore let my people know my name, therefore on that day, that I am He who says 'Here I am' " (Isa. 52:6), cannot be otherwise understood.

However, it appears that the message of the name never became actually popular in biblical Israel. It seems that the people did not accept the new vocalization. The interpretation, to be sure, hovers around the name in their consciousness; but it does not penetrate it. In the innermost nucleus it remains the dark, mysterious cry, and there is evidence in all periods until the days of the Talmud that an awareness of the sense of the pronoun "he" hidden in it was always present. The prohibition against pronouncing the name only raised an ancient reluctance, which was rooted in the resistance against rationalization, to the power of a taboo. Nevertheless a tremendous vitalization in the relation of the people to the name clearly took place on Sinai; the boys are given names containing it, and just as its proclamation combines with the moving and stopping of the crowd, so it also finds place in the life of the tribe and in that of the individual; the certainty of the presence of the God as a quality of His being began to possess the souls of the generations. It is impossible properly to grasp such a process independently of the actually unaccepted yet so effective message contained in the meaning of the name.

The meaning of the name is usually ascribed to the "Elohist," to whose source this section of the narrative is attributed. But quite apart from the fact that there was no Elohist in this sense and that, as has been said, if we eliminate complements and supplements, we find a uniform and firmly constructed narrative—such discoveries or conversions are not born at the writing desk. A speech like this *ehyeh asher ehyeh* does not belong to literature but to the sphere attained by the founders of religion. If it is theology, it is that archaic theology which, in the form of a historical narrative, stands at the threshold of every genuine historical religion. No matter who related that speech or when, he derived it from a tradition that, in the last resort, cannot go back to anybody other than the founder. What the latter revealed of his religious experience to his disciples we cannot know; that he informed them of what had happened to him we must assume; in any case, the origin of such a tradition cannot be sought anywhere else.

At his relatively late period Moses did not establish the religious relationship between the Bnei Israel and YHVH. He was not the first to utter that "primal sound" in enthusiastic astonishment. That may have been done by somebody long before who, driven by an irresistible force along a new road, now felt himself to be preceded along that road by "Him," the invisible one who permitted Himself to be seen. But it was Moses, who, on this religious relationship, established a covenant between the God and "His people." Nothing of such a kind can be imagined except on the assumption that a relation which had come down from ancient times has been melted in the fire of some new personal experience. The foundation takes place before the assembled host; the experience is undergone in solitude.

Holy Event (Exodus 19–27)

Martin Buber

We know nothing of Israel's religious situation in the Egyptian age, and we can only conjecture on the basis of scattered disconnected phrases (e.g., Ezek. 20:7f) that it was out of a state of religious decay that Moses stirred them up. We can proceed only by putting the period of the Exodus alongside that of the Fathers.

When we pass from the atmosphere of the patriarchal tradition, as we have tried to picture it hypothetically, and enter the atmosphere of the Exodus tradition, we are confronted at first glance with something new. But it is quickly manifest that this does not mean a change in the deity, but a change in men. We have already seen that the deity is in essence no other than the primitive diety. Against this the human partner is essentially changed; therefore, the situation common to the two is entirely different; and with this the sphere in which the deity acts is so different that one may easily think the very character of this activity to be changed, and one does not recognize the identity of the agent. The new thing from the human side is that here we have "people," not "a people" in the strictest sense, but at all events the element people. That is to say, this collection of men is no longer a company assembled around the recipients of revelation and their kinsmen as in the patriarchal age, but a something that is called "Israel" and which the deity can acknowledge to be "His people"—again it is not of decisive importance whether this people comprises all the tribes of Israel, or only some of them, the rest having been left in Canaan or having returned thither before this. We do not know whether "Israel"

From *On the Bible: Eighteen Studies by Martin Buber.* © 1968 by Schocken Books, Inc.

originally was the name of a people or the name of a "holy confederacy," to which the tribes were gathered together by the leadership of
Moses, and gave themselves, after their sacred call, the name "Israel,"
the meaning of which probably is not "God strives," but "God rules."

But if this is the original explanation of "Israel," then this community has already, in consequence of the special historical conditions,
reached, at the moment of the Exodus—i.e., at the moment when we
are able to perceive them historically—that stage of self-evident
unitedness, so that we are justified in applying to them the name
"people," even though they do not yet possess all the marks reckoned
as belonging to this concept. And if "Israel" was already in origin the
name of a people, then it is only at this point, at the exodus from
Egypt, not in Egypt itself, that the people comes into actual existence,
and only at this point is the name "Israel" perfectly manifest as "the
visible program of God's sovereignty." And the deity now acts historically upon this people seen by Him as an absolute unity, the same deity
whom the Fathers discovered as the guardian God accompanying
them. The change that we think we perceive in Him as we now
advance in time is nothing but the transformation of the situation into
a historical one, and the greatness of Moses consists in the fact that he
accepts the situation and exhausts its possibilities. No external influence
is to be found here. Indeed it is vain to attempt to find here a Kenite
ingredient; YHVH has taken over nothing from the Egyptian god Aton,
who is brought into the picture as "monotheistic"; and other things
which may have approached Him have not touched His nature. This
God has become manifest as a God of history, because He became the
God of Israel, this Israel that only now came into being, that only now
He was able to "find" (Hos. 9:10), and because this Israel only now has
entered the realm of history. He reveals Himself to it: what was hidden
in prehistoric time is made historically manifest. Our path in the
history of faith is not a path from one kind of deity to another, but in
fact a path from the "God who hides Himself" (Isa. 45:15) to the One
that reveals Himself.

If we look at the first of the writing prophets, Amos, and examine
the traditions that he handles concerning this activity of YHVH, and ask:
what are the reminiscences that he knows to be common to all his
hearers, these two appear before us: the leading from Egypt through
the desert (Amos 2:10; 3:1; 9:7), and the appropriation the deity expresses in a word reminiscent of the marriage union (Gen. 4:1) but
later uses to indicate the primal mission of the prophet (Jer. 1:5), "you

have I known" (Amos 3:2). The first of these two, talked over by everyone and thought to be understood by all—"I have brought you up" (2:10)—Amos shows (9:7) to be something that is in no way peculiar to Israel, but the fundamental fact of the historic contact of this leader God with the peoples. It is with set purpose that record is here kept of the names of the two neighboring peoples who fought most mightily with all Israel or Judah, the one in early times, the other in the immediate past. In these instances, very painful as they are to you—this is the force of the prophet's words—you see that this God of yours, of whose historic dealing with you you boast, deals historically with other peoples as with you, leading each of them on its wanderings and singling out its lot. The second thing, not familiar to the people as to its expression and sense, but corresponding in the people's memory to the events of revelation and convenant making, he lays bare as the *suprahistorical election* to be bound absolutely, peculiar "only" to Israel alone among all the peoples: "therefore"—and now comes the iron word from the Decalogue—"I will ordain upon you all your iniquities." YHVH has not revealed Himself to any other family of "the families of the earth" save only to this Israel, and to them He has revealed Himself really as the "zealous God." And in the mouth of Amos's contemporary, Hosea, who presupposes no general thought or teaching, but expresses directly the things of the heart, YHVH illustrates His zealousness by His experience with Israel in the desert: I loved (11:1) and they betrayed me (9:10; 11:2; 13:6).

Those Semitic peoples who call their tribal deities by the name *malk,* meaning originally counsellor, arbitrator, leader, and only afterwards receiving the meaning of king, appear to have expressed by this name not the oracle power of the settlement but the leadership in primitive wanderings and conquest. These are nomad gods, leader gods of the tribe which, through the political change of meaning of the word, become afterwards "kings"; the type of this tribal god, although not the name, we find in the message of Jephthah to the king of the "Ammonites" (or more correctly the king of Moab), where he tells him that Chemosh his god "disinherited" other peoples even as YHVH had done, in order to give a land to the people led by him (Judg. 11:23f). Amos's saying about the bringing up of the Aramaeans disposes of such a notion: the peoples do not know who is their liberator, they each call him by a different name, each one thinks to have one of its own, whereas we know the One, because He "has known" us. This is the *national* universalism of the prophetic faith.

The Mosaic age does not possess this religious view of the history of peoples, but it does have the fundamental religious experience that opens the door to this view. What is preserved for us here is to be regarded not as the "historization" of a myth or of a cult drama, nor is it to be explained as the transposition of something originally beyond time into historical time: a great history-faith does not come into the world through interpretation of the extrahistorical as historical, but by receiving an occurrence experienced as a "wonder," that is, as an event that cannot be grasped except as an act of God. Something happens to us, the cause of which we cannot ascribe to our world; the event has taken place just now, we cannot understand it, we can only believe it (Exod. 14:31). It is a holy event. We acknowledge the performer (15:1, 21): "I will sing unto YHVH, for He has verily risen, the horse and its rider He has cast into the sea."

In this undeniably contemporary song the deliverance is asserted as a holy event. A later song, which nevertheless is very ancient in form, vocabulary, and sentence construction, the song framing "the Blessing of Moses," praises in its first half (the second half tells of the conquest of the land) a series of divine appearances in the wilderness, beginning with the appearance at Mount Sinai. From the difficult text it can be understood that the "holy ones" of the people collect around YHVH, when they camp "at His feet" (cf. Exod. 24:10); that later the people receive from the divine words the "instruction" (torah + which Moses "commands"; that so "the congregation of Jacob" becomes YHVH's "inheritance"; and that finally the heads of the tribes gather together and proclaim YHVH to be king over them. What is recorded here of the holy event can only be reconstructed incompletely out of the exodus story. The fact that the proclamation is lacking here is probably to be explained by the fear they felt for the influence, combated by the prophets, of the melekh cult of the neighboring peoples, that is to say, for the penetration of child sacrifice into Israel. Isaiah is the first (6:5) directly to give YHVH the title melekh, king, after forcibly demonstrating the uncleanness of the people over against Him. But we still have preserved for us another echo of the proclamation, namely the last verse of the Song of the Sea (Exod. 15:18), which although it is not so near in time to the event as the opening of the Song, yet clearly is "not long after the event about which it tells." Here proclamation is made triumphantly that the divine kingdom will stand forever. This is to be understood not in the light of the state concept of kingship, nor on the basis of the later idea of a cosmic-cultic kingdom of God, but only as the recognition by wandering tribes of their divine leader: the sovereignty of this leader over His people is proclaimed.

Thus over against the two sayings of Amos we have before us two series of events. The first comprises the deliverance from Egypt and the leading through the wilderness to Canaan, the second comprises the revelation, the making of the covenant and the setting up of an order of the people by the leadership of the divine *melekh*. That is to say, the first series exists for the sake of the second. So we are to understand the words "unto me" in the first Sinai message (Exod. 19:4), which still precedes the revelation in the thunderstorm. YHVH bears the people, as the eagle from time to time bears one of its young on its wing (a late form of the picture is found in Deut. 32:11), to the place of revelation: if the people hearken to the voice that now speaks to them, they will become for YHVH, whose is all the earth, a "peculiar treasure" among all the peoples that are His: they will become for Him, the king, a "king's realm" (cf. 2 Sam. 3:28), surrounding Him near at hand and serving Him directly, a circle of *kohanim,* that is "foremost ones at the king's hand" (so 1 Chron. 18:17 calls the office, while 2 Sam. 8:18 gives it the name *kohanim,* meaning those who minister to the king), a "holy" (i.e., hallowed, set apart for Him) *goy* (i.e., body of people). The saying dates apparently from the time before the division of the Israelite kingdom, and it is already influenced by the political changes of meaning in the concept *melekh;* but it is clear that a traditional basic view of the meaning of the events, the Exodus and the making of the covenant, became crystallized in it. YHVH acts as *melekh* in the sense of sovereign. So through a holy event there comes into existence this category, decisive from the point of view of the history of faith, of the "holy people," the hallowed body of people, as image and claim; at a later time, after the people had broken the covenant again and again, this category changed and was replaced by the messianic promise and hope.

Both series of events are blended together in a most noteworthy way in the great holy object, indeed the greatest of all holy objects created by the "nomadic faith," the faith of a people seeking a land and believing in the divine leader, who brings them to it, namely the Ark. It clearly cannot be dated any later; for there is to be found in it all the incentive and motive force of the holy adventure, all its symbol-begetting power. And in spite of the many parallels in the history of religion to one or other aspect of the ark, it can hardly be maintained that the ark is borrowed from anywhere, for its nature lies precisely in the unity of these different aspects. It carries the cherub throne of the Lord who, seated thereon, guides the wandering and the battle (here both are still absolutely interconnected the one with the other); and together with this is the ark proper containing the tablets. These are called "the testimony," because it is by them that the covenant is always attested anew, and so the ark is also called "the Ark of the Covenant." Neither of the two could be wanting. This holy object is a visible unity of the two divine activities: the activity of the leader, who now, in the historic situation, has become also "a man of war" (Exod. 15:3), and the activity of the revealer, whose revelation, once it had taken place, is never more to be concealed and hidden, but must remain carved on stone or written on a scroll. At the same time even this characteristically is not attached to a place: the tablets are fixed in the ark, but the ark is by nature mobile, moving in the tent and outside it, for it is forbidden to remove the poles (25:15). Even after the ark stands compact in the temple in Jerusalem, they are not removed (1 Kings 8:8); but this means only reverence for tradition and symbolism, and not any longer a direct notion of the leader deity. The double call, originating in the wilderness (Num. 10:35f.), to the Lord of the ark, who travels and halts with the camp, "rise up YHVH" and "return YHVH" and the "melekh shout" because Israel's God is "with him" (23:21), is no more heard. His special name "YHVH of hosts" (i.e., the host of the people and the host of heaven, concerning both of which the Song of Deborah speaks) is still in the mouth of the people, but its real meaning is no longer really known—until Amos comes and expounds it again.

The paradox on which the sanctity of the ark is based (every "holy" thing is founded on a paradox) is this: that an invisible deity becomes perceptible as One who comes and goes. According to tradition, as far as we can still recognize it, the ark must be brought into the "tent of meeting"—not the tent that is described in all its parts in Scripture, and which really cannot be conceived in the wilderness, but the tent of the leader ("the tent" of Exod. 33:7ff.)—after atonement for sin had been made. The images of the calf, which has no other design than to be a likeness of that very God "who brought you up from the land of Egypt" (32:4), was put up to make the leadership permanently perceptible. In the hour of forgiveness God grants (33:14, 17) that His "face" will go with the people. The meaning of this is that a visibleness is conceded which in fact is none; that is to say, not the visibleness of an "image" or a "shape" (20:4), but as in the vision of the ancients

(24:10) the visibleness of a *place.* This is the hour in which the holy object is born. Later, men attempted to render the principle, which could no longer be reconstructed in its reality, more conceivable by means of a concept of the *kabod,* that is, the fiery "weight" or "majesty" of the God radiating from the invisible, which now "fills" again and again the "dwelling" of the tent (40:34), just as it had "taken dwelling" upon the mount (24:16). In truth this idea of a filling of the tent, so that Moses "cannot come into the tent of meeting" (40:35), contradicts its character and purpose. The true tent—formerly Moses' leader tent, and now that of the leader deity—is characterized by just this: that Moses enters it for the sake of "meeting" the deity, and that "everyone who seeks YHVH" (33:7) can hand over his petition to Moses, who will talk it over with the deity. It is of the essence of the leadership that there is the divine word in dialogue: informative and initiative speaking. The informative function passes afterwards from the divine speech to the oracle vessels called *Urim and Tummim,* and from the *nabi*—for as such the former writing prophets know Moses from tradition (Hos. 12:13)—to the priest. Whereas the initiative speech, the genuine speech of the leader which is no answer but a commission and a command, is henceforth also spoken only to the *nabi,* whom "the hand" seizes and sends. Kings rule, priests minister in their office, while the man of the Spirit, without power or office, hears the word of his leader.

Besides the movable divine abode, yet another feature of the nomadic period has entered into the life of the settled community, and so deeply that it persisted long after the age of the settlement and shared the subsequent wanderings of the people in all ages and generations, becoming almost a perpetual renewal of the first event: the feast of the Passover. A nomadic feast, as it certainly was in primitive times, it was transformed by the holy event into a feast of history; but that which recurs in the festival is the act of going forth, the beginning of the journeyings; the nomadic feast, without any historical character, becomes the historical feast. With loins girt, with feet shod, and with staff in hand, in the haste of departure they eat the sacrifice (Exod. 12:11). The Israelites do what was done formerly, not only performing the action, but in the performance doing it. Through the length and breadth of history, in every new home in a strange land, on this night the stimulus of the God-guided wanderings is active again, and history happens. The Israelites recount the story of the feast, this story that "cannot be the literary product of a later source," but which "contains facts," "solid tradition, springing from the ground of historic events." But it is not the purpose to recount only what happened there and then. On the night of the Passover "the assembled company is fused together in every year and in all the world with the first cult confederates and attains that unity, which existed formerly at the first occasion in Egypt." As they who keep the covenant in life know it to be the covenant that "YHVH our God made with us in Horeb," "not with our fathers," but "with us our very selves here this day, all of us being alive" (Deut. 5:2f.), so telling the story of God's leading they experience His historic deed as occurring to themselves. In His footsteps they are wakeful through the night, which was a night of watching for YHVH and is now a night of watching for all the children of Israel in their generations (Exod. 12:42).

Berith, covenant, between YHVH and Israel denotes an expansion of the leadership and the following so as to cover every department of the people's life. The fundamental relationship represented perceptibly, that the deity—and it is the same in whatever form (pillar of fire, etc.) or even in no form (ark, "face")—goes before the company of wanderers and they follow after Him, and know in their heart that His way is the right way, this relationship is now taken as an all-embracing relationship founded as an everlasting bond in the making of the covenant. Here the mutual character of this relationship is announced, but the people feel already that a covenant with such a deity as this means no legal agreement, but a surrender to the divine power and grace. The most sublime expression of this is given in two sayings of YHVH (3:14 and 33:19), which by their sentence structure are shown to belong to each other (two similar verbal forms linked by the word *asher,* meaning "whoever," "whomever"). The first says that indeed the deity is always present but in every given hour in the appearance that pleases Him; that is to say, He does not allow Himself to be limited to any form of revelation and He does not limit Himself to any of them. And the second says that He bestows His grace and mercy on whom He will, and lets no one order a criterion for Him nor Himself orders any. But connected with this is that element called YHVH's "demonism," the dread of which overcomes us whenever we read about YHVH meeting Moses, His chosen and sent one, and "seeking to kill him" (4:24). This is no survival, no "primitive fiend" that has entered, as it were, by mistake from earlier polydemonism into this purer sphere, but it is of the essential stuff of early biblical piety, and without it the later form cannot be understood. The diety claims the chosen one or his dearest possession, falls upon him in order to set him free afterwards as a "blood bridegroom," as a man betrothed and set apart for Him by his blood. This is the most ancient revelation of grace: the true grace is the grace of death, a gracing; man owes himself to the deity from the beginning. And here too, as with Jacob (Gen. 32), the event is significantly linked with a journey ordered earlier: the wanderer has to go through the dangerous meeting, in order to attain the final grace of the leader God.

The idea of following the deity raises itself—no longer in the Mosaic but still in an early biblical age—to the idea of imitating the deity, notably in the interpretation of the greatest institution set up by Moses, the Sabbath. It appears that the Sabbath too was not created *ex nihilo,* although its origin is not yet clear. It is certain that the material used for this institution was adopted by a mighty force of faith, recast and molded into an indestructible creation of the life of the faithful. It is impossible to think of an age later than that of Moses in which this could have happened. Many think the "ethical Decalogue" (Exod. 20) to be later than the "cultic" (34), but the latter was its harvest and pilgrimage feasts presupposes an agricultural usage, whereas the former is yet "timeless," not yet stamped with any particular organized form of human society; the "cultic" is seen after detailed examination to be a "secondary mixture," whereas the "ethical" in its fundamental core is known to have a primary, "apodictic" character. The Sabbath ordinance contained in it, in the original shorter version—beginning apparently with the word "remember" and continuing as far as "thy God"—is the ordinance of setting apart the seventh day for YHVH (that is to say, a day not ordered for cultic reasons, but freed of all authority of command except that of the one Lord). On this day men do not do, as on other days, "any work"; the meaning of this for the nomad shepherd, for the shepherd who cannot neglect his flock, is that he puts off all "jobs which he can do today or leave to tomorrow," that he interrupts the cultivation of land in the oasis, that he does not journey to new places of pasture, and so on. It is only in the age of the settlement that the Sabbath becomes a strict day of rest. Among the established and illustrative sayings that come up for consideration (we find in the Pentateuch seven variants of the ordinance), two are of special importance: Exod. 23:12, and 31:12ff. It is customary to connect them with different "sources" from different periods, but a very rare verb (which is only found elsewhere in the Bible once, in the apparently contemporaneous story of Absalom, 2 Sam. 16:14), meaning "to draw one's breath," links the two, the "social" and the "religious" motives, in true biblical repetitive style, referring to one another and explaining one another. The one says that the purpose of the Sabbath ordinance was that the beast might rest and that men whose work is obligatory (that is to say, the slave and the hireling sojourner), who *must needs* work all the week, might draw breath. The other passage, which sets out the Sabbath ordinance in the most solemn form and imposes the death penalty upon those who transgress it, belongs in the original core of its first part (vv. 13–15 in a shorter version) to the species of ordinances in the "apodictical style" of which A. Alt writes. Having examined them fundamentally in their typical difference from all the rest of the later Canaanite-influenced "casuistical" forms, he rightly says "that the rise of this species was possible when the bond-relationship to YHVH and the resulting institution of making and renewing the covenant with Him came into being." But to this part of the ordinance is added a second, obviously a later expansion, in which the Sabbath is designated as an "everlasting covenant" and a "sign for ever," "for in six days YHVH made the heaven and the earth, and on the seventh day He rested and drew breath." The crass anthropomorphism binds together the deity and the tired, exhausted slave, and with words arousing the soul calls the attention of the free man's indolent heart to the slave; but at the same time it sets up before the community the loftiest sense of following the leader. Everyone that belongs to the essence of Israel—and the servants, the sojourners included, belong to it—shall be able to imitate YHVH without hindrance.

"The sayings in the apodictic form," says Alt, "mostly have to do with things with which casuistic law did not deal at all, and by its secular nature could not deal. For the question is here on the one hand the sacred sphere of the contact with the divine world . . . and on the other hand holy realms in men's life together . . . religion, morals, and law are here still unseparated together." And again, "in Israel's apodictic law an aggressive, as yet quite unbroken force operates, a force which subjects every realm of life to the absolute authority claim of YHVH's will for His people, and therefore cannot recognize any secular or neutral zone." These words fit our view that YHVH as "God of Israel" does not become the lord of a cultic order of faith, shut up within itself, but the lord of an order of people including all spheres of life, that is to say a *melekh,* and a *melekh* taking his authority seriously— unlike the gods of other tribes. I do not at all mean to go too far beyond Alt's carefully weighed thesis and to connect with Sinai the whole series of these sayings, rhythmically constructed in order to engrave them upon the memory of the people, among which there recurs again and again the "I" of the speaking God, and the "thou" of the hearing Israel; but in those too that bear the distinct scent of the field about them, we feel that the fiery breath of Sinai has yet blown upon them. They are fragments of a people's order subject to the divine sovereignty.

As with the term "divine sovereignty" the meaning here is not a specialized religious authority but a sovereignty operating on all the reality of the community life, so with the term "people's order" the meaning is not the order of an indefinite society but of a completely definite people. To what is called in the Song of Deborah and in other ancient passages of Scripture "people of YHVH" a secular concept can approximate, namely the concept of "a true people," that is, a people that realizes in its life the basic meaning of the concept *am*, "people," of living one *im*, "with," another; it approximates to it although, to be sure, it does not actually reach it. The "social" element in the apodictic laws is to be understood not on the basis of the task of bettering the living conditions of society, but on the basis of establishing a true people, as the covenant partner of the *melekh*, according as the tribes are a people as yet only by God's act and not by their own. If, for example, it is ordered (Exod. 22:21) not to afflict the widow and orphan, or (22:20; 23:9) not to oppress the sojourner—here there is word about individuals dependent on others, lacking security, subject to the might of the mighty; but the aim of such commands is not the single person, but the "people of YHVH," this people that shall rise, but cannot rise so long as the social distance loosens the connections of the members of the people and decomposes their direct contact with one another. The *melekh* YHVH does not want to rule a crowd, but a community. There is already recognizable here, as in a network of roots, the widespread prophetic demand for social righteousness, which reached its highest peak in the promise of the union of the peoples in a confederacy of mankind through the mediation of the "servant" from Israel (Isa. 42:1–6).

Hence we see that the agricultural statute with its ordinances for the periodical interruption of the families' privilege of eating the fruits of their allotted ground, the remission of debts in the sabbatical year, and the leveling of all possessions in the year of Jubilee, is only late with regard to the literary setting before us (Lev. 25), whereas with regard to its contents it presents "a transposition of the patriarchal conditions of the wilderness age to the agricultural conditions of Palestine," and is designed so that "the absolute coherence of the people" will live on in the consciousness of the common possession of land. This common ownership is by its nature God's property, as we know from ancient Arabic parallels, and the undeniably early saying "Mine is the land, for you are sojourners and settlers with me" (v. 23) expresses the ancient claim of the divine leader on the ways of land-seeking and land-conquest, His claim to all the land of settlement. We have already seen above how in the patriarchal story the divine name was called as of their true owner upon the places occupied beforehand in Canaan, as the names of their owners are called upon the great estates (Ps. 49:12). The divine ownership of the ground and the whole people's possession of it originate in a unity meant to last forever, whereas the rights of the individual are only conditional and temporary.

Within the ancient people's order, as we can deduce it from the apodictic laws, we find the sacred sphere of contact with the divine world substantially "only in the sense of keeping away all practices directed to gods or spirits other than YHVH, or implying a misuse of things belonging to Him and therefore holy, as for example His name or the Sabbath." Only a single short sacrificial statute (Exod. 20, 24ff.) can be cited here in its original form, purified of additions. The words, "in every place, where I cause my name to be remembered, I will come unto thee and bless thee" come from the true character of the ancient nomad deity who does not allow Himself to be kept to any mountain or temple. Sacrifices were apparently not customary in the wilderness apart from the nomadic offering of the firstborn of the flock (13:12; 34:19), except in extraordinary situations (the joining of Kenites, the ratification of the Sinai covenant). And there appears to have been no fixed sacrificial cult with special sacrificial rules; Amos was probably following a reliable tradition in this connection (5:25), although he gave it an extreme interpretation.

But there is one more feature belonging to this *melekh* covenant between God and people, this leading and following, and that is the person of the mediator. The revelation, the making of the covenant, the giving of the statutes, was performed by the "translating" utterance of a mortal man; the queries and requests of the people are presented by the internal or external words of this person; the species of man that bears the word from above downwards and from below upwards is called *nabi*, announcer. So Hosea (12:14) calls Moses. In the earlier parts of the Pentateuch Moses is not so designated directly; in a remarkable story (Num. 12) an ancient verse inserted in it (6b–8a) sets Moses apparently above the *nebiim:* for they only know the deity by visions, whereas to Moses, "His servant," He speaks "mouth to mouth" (not mouth to ear, but really mouth to mouth "inspiring"; cf. also Exod. 33:11, "face to face as when a man speaks to his neighbor"), and moreover not in riddles, which a man must still explain, but so that the hearing of the utterance is itself a "sight" of the intention. And this just fits the concept of the *nabi,* known also in a later verse of the Pentateuch (Exod. 7:1; cf. 4:16), where the "god" who speaks into a person is, so to say, dependent on the *nabi* who speaks out. It is relatively unimportant when this term came into existence, but it is important that the thing is as old as Israel. In the story, composed out of the saga material in a strictly consistent form, we are told in a particularly manifold repetition of the roots *ra'ah, hazah* (to see) (Gen. 12:1, 7; 13:14, 15; 15:1; 17:1; 18:1, 2a, 2b), of the series of visions Abraham saw, until he became the mediator between below and above, an undismayed mediator, pleading with God (18:25), who now declares him to be a *nabi* (20:7); in this story the prevailing view in prophetic circles of the antiquity of prophecy is obviously expressed. The temporary sequence seer-prophet recalls an ancient note on word changes, which tells us more than mere word history (1 Sam. 9:9). At all events no age in the history of early Israelite faith can be understood historically without considering as active therein this species of man with his mission and function, his declaration and mediation. Whatever else Moses is and does, his prophecy, his ministry of the word, is the crystal center of his nature and work. It is true, he does not "prophesy," the prophetic mission in the strict sense belonging to a later and different situation between God and people, but he does everything a prophet should in this early situation: he represents the Lord, he enunciates the message, and commands in His name.

Here we meet a problem, which historically, both in the spiritual and the political sense, is singularly important. The divine *melekh* leads the *qahal,* the assembly of the men, by means of the one favored and called by Him, the bearer of the "charismatic" power, the power of grace. This power, however, is not based, as with oriental kings, upon the myth of divine birth or adoption, but upon the utterly unmythical secret of the personal election and vocation, and is not hereditary. After the man's death it is necessary to wait until the *ruah,* the stormy breath ("spirit") of the deity, rushes into another man. (Of the transmission of the visible charisma, the "splendor," or part of it, to a man "in whom there is spirit" Scripture speaks only once, that is concerning the transmission of Moses to "his servant" Joshua, Num. 27: 15ff. The doubtful character of this passage increased later considerably with the insertion of the *Urim* as a determining power of leadership, 21f.) Because of this, the commission and therefore the actual leadership discontinues, a break that in the time of the conquest served the seminomads ill, for even without this they were given to unlimited family and tribal particularism, loosening the YHVH confederation and weakening "Israel's" power of action. Joshua's attempt to secure the continued unity of the people, by getting rid of the family idols and by founding a tribal amphictyony around a cult-directed center only, succeeded but partially, as can be seen from the Song of Deborah. The divine *melekh*, who wishes to determine the whole life of the community, is not content to be substituted by a cult deity, to whom it is sufficient to offer sacrifice at the yearly pilgrimages. The Sinai enthusiasm for the absolute God grows again and expresses itself in the activity and song of the Deborah circle. But the increasing difficulties of accomplishing the as yet incomplete conquest and of strengthening a position against the hostile neighbors arouse in opposition to this theopolitical ardor a "realist-political" movement, aimed at establishing the hereditary charisma known to Israel from the great powers, the dynastic securing of continuity. The opposition of the faithful to the *melekh* arises especially strongly in the days of Gideon, whose refusal to accept the royal crown may be regarded as historically true. But already his son Abimelech stands in the opposite camp. And a national catastrophe, which the people may be inclined to see as a defeat of the leader God Himself, occurs; on the battlefield of Ebenezer the victorious Philistines capture the Ark of the Covenant which went at the head of the Israelite host (1 Sam. 4). This hour represents the turning point in the history of Israelite faith.

Exodus 1–4 / The Prologue to the Exodus Cycle

Michael Fishbane

In the Book of Exodus, the several groups of ancestors which were recorded in the Book of Genesis as the sons of Jacob-Israel (Gen. 35:23–26; 46:8–27) are transformed into a nation: the sons/people of Israel. The process is gradual and deliberate. The genealogy of Jacob and his clan, recorded in Gen. 46:8–27, is repeated in Exod. 1:1–5, so that a link is forged between it and the preceding patriarchal narratives. Indeed, the transitional function of this genealogy can best be appreciated from a structural point of view: the last verse in the Book of Genesis, Gen. 50:26 ("Then Joseph died at 110 years, and they embalmed him so that he was encased in a mummy in Egypt"), is recapitulated in Exod. 1:6 ("Then Joseph died, together with his brethren and that entire generation"), thereby framing the intervening genealogy. With the resumption of the plot line, the "sons of Israel" of verse 1 are called "the *nation* of the sons of Israel" in verse 9. The stage is thus set for the national epic of liberation which follows.

The Books of Genesis and Exodus are linked not only by this stress on ethnic continuity but by thematic considerations as well. Joseph, on his deathbed, tells his sons that "Elohim will surely *remember* you and bring you up from this land to the land which He foreswore to Abraham, Isaac, and Jacob" (Gen. 50:25). This promise is alluded to at an early point in Exodus: When the Israelites suffered from the travail of their Egyptian bondage, "Elohim *remembered*" His covenantal promise to the patriarchs (2:24). This promise and remembrance are

From *Text and Texture: Close Readings of Biblical Texts.* © 1979 by Schocken Books, Inc.

again referred to in the traditions recording Moses' initial encounters with the ancestral God of the patriarchs (cf. Exod. 3:16–17 with Gen. 50:25, and Exod. 6:3–5 with Exod. 2:23–26), so that the divine appearances to Moses are also linked to the chain of promises to the patriarchs in Genesis.

Another more striking link between Genesis and Exodus is provided by the oracle of Gen. 15:13–15, which announces a considerable delay in the fulfillment of the divine promises of the inheritance of Canaan. According to this oracle prophecy, Abraham's seed would first be a dweller (*ger*) in a land not their own (i.e. Egypt), where they would also be enslaved (*va'avadum*) and tormented (*ve'innu*) for four hundred years. Thereupon, the oracle concludes, Israel would leave that land—Egypt—and return "here" (i.e., to Canaan). These themes and this language are echoed in the opening chapters of Exodus, as if to alert the reader that the preconditions set by the Genesis oracle are now being realized. Hence, one reads that the Egyptians enslaved (*vaya'avidu*, 1:13) the Israelites, and tormented them (*'anoto*, 1:11); that Moses named his son Gershom, for "I have become a dweller (*ger*) in a foreign land" (2:22); and that God promised the Israelites the riches of Egypt (3:22), even as had been foretold in Gen. 15:14.

Considerable literary effort was thus expended to link the patriarchal histories of Genesis with the Egyptian sojourn of Exodus. Moreover, the last example, which foreshadows the termination of Israelite servitude by allusions to the oracle in Genesis, brings us to the main concern of the present chapter. The opening chapters of the Book of Exodus (1–4) will be shown to foreshadow the events and scenarios of chapters 5–19. To fully appreciate this stylization of the ancient record, Exodus 1–19 must be seen for what it is: a literary construct fusing saga and history.

The exodus from Egypt was experienced as an event of divine redemption, during which ancient promises were realized and divine power confirmed. The transformative nature of this event in the lives of the ancient Israelites affected its recollection and literary formulation. For those who experienced it, no simple chronological report would do justice to the wonder of the divine intervention in their historical lives. Only the saga form would do, focusing selectively on specific events and people, endowing the encounters between the principal actors with a paradigmatic cast, and infusing historical process with the wonder of supernatural events.

Seen in this light, Exodus 1–19 is a presentation of the "events" of the Egyptian bondage and liberation through the prism of religious memory and imagination. The biblical focus is, accordingly, on divine power and will, on human hope and intransigence, on Moses and the Israelites, on Pharaoh and the Egyptians. Factual details become secondary to a dramatization of the inner conviction that with the exodus-event the God of the patriarchs has fulfilled His ancient promises. The narrative style is cast in a rhythm of alternating plagues and dialogues, so that the pace of events has a liturgical, climactic effect. The mystery and forms of divine providence are ever present, foreshadowing events to come.

The opening depiction of the Israelites in Exodus 1 sets the tone: "And the Israelites were fruitful and plentiful; they multiplied and became very powerful until the land was filled with them" (v. 7). This situation—which has the overtones of a new creation and beginning—is reemphasized by Pharaoh's corresponding assertion: "Behold, the Israelites have become more numerous and powerful than we" (v. 9). To keep his control over them he institutes two measures of population control, both of which backfire. First the Israelites are forced to build store-cities. "But the more they were oppressed the more they increased and spread" (v. 12). The second measure is even more drastic: infanticide. According to the Pharaoh's decree, all firstborn male Israelites are to be killed. However, because of the resourcefulness and piety of the midwives (v. 17), the Israelites were able to avert this danger and so increase in number that the Pharaoh was impelled to reissue and stiffen his earlier decree: "Every newborn male must be thrown into the Nile, although every female may be kept alive" (v. 22).

All these events set the backdrop for the hero Moses. Hidden in an ark, and thereby saved from the calamitous decree, Moses is drawn forth alive from the waters of the Nile (2:1–10).

With the rescue of Moses, the scene shifts abruptly. Once singled out, the hero immediately assumes his historical destiny. Time is telescoped, actions are highly stylized, and Moses is portrayed from the start as linking his personal fate to that of his people. Thus "Moses grew up, went out to meet his brethren, and saw their toil" (2:11). Shortly thereafter, he intervenes in a fight to save a fellow Israelite and kills the offending Egyptian. When tauntingly called a "prince and judge" of his people, Moses flees to the desert, thereby counterpointing with his freedom the servitude of the Israelites who yet remain in Egypt:

> The Israelites groaned on account of their labor and called out;
> and their cry for help from their labor went up to Elohim.
> Elohim heard their tormented plea, and Elohim remembered
> his covenant with Abraham, Isaac, and Jacob. And so Elohim
> looked upon the Israelites, and Elohim took heed.
>
> (vv. 23–25)

With this, the opening chapters conclude: the historical servitude has been described, the hero has been introduced and involved, and God Himself—up until now silent—"took heed."

At this point the narrative, which remains with Moses in the Midianite steppeland, takes a decisive turn. While shepherding his flock, and undoubtedly mindful of the oppression of his brethren enslaved in Egypt, Moses sees a messenger of YHWH near a mountain, at a *sneh*-bush, seemingly enveloped—but unconsumed—by fire. Moses, his daily rhythm disrupted, is addressed: "Remove your sandals from your feet because you are standing on holy ground" (3:5). The event is a theophany of the God of Abraham, Isaac, and Jacob. The promised redemption is now at hand.

The mountain remains a mountain, and the bush a bush. But now all is changed: God has spoken to Moses. The words do not arise from within Moses. To the contrary; he is confronted and commanded by them. "He said: 'Moses, Moses,' and he said: 'Here I am [*hinneni*].' " This address and response hark back to God's earlier speech to Abraham before his final trial (22:1). At the moment of divine address, Moses, like Abraham before him, can only respond with his total presence and submit to its claim over his life. To be sure, he has been preparing for this moment his whole mature life. Indeed, before fleeing Egypt, he had even "acted out" on the body of a taskmaster the liberation and justice that the times required. Now, when God appears to him to fulfill the promise to the patriarchs (vv. 6–8), Moses knows that he can never again return to his prior everyday activities. God's revelatory presence has driven a wedge into his lifetime and that of his brethren. His own personal past—where private passion for justice had only produced a random act of resentment—is over.

The divine revelation and new promise thus mark a transformation in Moses' religious consciousness. He is to be a messenger of God to his people (v. 10). But, overcome with insignificance and fear, he balks: "Who am I that I should go to Pharaoh and that I should deliver the Israelites from Egypt?" (v. 11). Moses knows what has to be done for God's sake, and for his own integrity. But he fears the cost. He has to surrender his "I," his sense of self, to God's will and command. Sensing this, God responds to Moses' repeated "I's" of verse 11 with: "I shall be ['ehyeh] with you" (v. 12). And to further strengthen his will, He gives Moses a sign "that I have sent you" (v. 12). This sign is the promise that He would bring him back to this spot after the exodus event.

But as such a sign was for the future, Moses then asks this God to reveal His name—so that the people to whom he will go will be convinced in the immediate present (v. 13). The sequence and meaning of the ensuing passage (vv. 14–15) are, in the preserved tradition, somewhat garbled; and so scholars have naturally offered many interpretations. Be this as it may, the following point may be underscored. Before the name YHWH is revealed in verse 15 to Moses as the name of the ancient God of the patriarchs, a midrashic play on this name is given (v. 14)—a "play" of profound theological seriousness, since it serves to characterize this God through His name. God says to Moses that He is 'ehyeh 'asher 'ehyeh, "I shall be that which I shall be," and that he (Moses) should tell the people, " 'ehyeh (I shall be) has sent me to you" (v. 14). No more, we seem to be cautioned, may be ascribed to God than that. He is the Unconditioned One who shall be as He shall be.

But the Israelites have first to undergo a spiritual transformation in order to trust the words of Moses on behalf of YHWH. Sensing this difficulty—and probably to assure himself as well—Moses requests and receives three new signs from God: his staff could be transformed into a snake, his hand could become leprous, and the Nile waters could be turned to blood (4:1–9). When Moses later shows these signs to the Israelites, the nation "trusted" (vayya'amen) that God had come to redeem His people from their suffering (4:31).

But even after God provides him with supplementary signs to convince the Israelites of his mission, Moses continues to express ambivalence about his task (4:10ff.). He does not question the task itself or its necessity, but he does question his own worthiness. God knows that this apparent humility and lack of self-confidence are a disguised lack of trust in divine providence, and He becomes furious. But Moses' renewed protestation of inability (4:10–16) supplements the earlier one (3:11) and further underscores the "prophetic" dimension of Moses' commission:

> Then Moses said to YHWH; "O my lord, surely I am not a man of words, nor was I yesterday or the day before that, even from the time when You spoke to your servant; but I am heavy of speech and heavy of tongue." But YHWH said to him: "Who gives a man speech, or makes him dumb, or deaf, or sighted, or blind? Is it not me, YHWH? Therefore, go now and I will be with your mouth, and instruct you what to speak." And he said: "Oh my Lord, send someone else." Then YHWH became enraged at Moses, and said: "What about your brother, Aaron the Levite? He speaks easily and is coming to you, and will be glad to see you. So speak to him and I will put the words in his mouth: I will be with your mouth and with his mouth, and will instruct you both what to do. He shall speak for you to the people. He will be as your mouth, and you will be to him as a god."

In this passage, Moses is presented as a prophet, who, like the ideal stated in Deut. 18:18, has divine words put into his mouth. A prophet is but a vessel, a "formulator" of the divine will that surges to earthly realization through him. Does not God say to Jeremiah that He would be with him and put His words into his mouth (Jer. 1:9)? And does He not also say to Jeremiah that "you will be like my mouth" (15:19)? But Moses resists the divine charge, so that, in the end, God says that Aaron will serve him (Moses) as a prophetic mouthpiece.

The two commission and resistance scenes of chapters 3 and 4 would seem to be alternate but complementary literary expressions of one transformative period in Moses' life. Taken together, the following structure of Moses' commission emerges:

1. God speaks (3:4–8)
2. Commission and sending (3:9–10)
3. The prophet resists, claiming to be unworthy and incompetent to be the messenger (3:11; 4:10)
4. God says that He will be with him and his speech (3:12; 4:11–12)
5. The prophet wants signs, or assurances, to bolster his spirit and/or convince those he is charged to address (3:12; 4:1–9).

Comparison of the literary formulation of Moses' commission with that of other prophets reveals instructive parallels:

Exodus 3–4	Isaiah	Jeremiah	Ezekiel
1. Encounter with God	6:1–4	1:5	2:1–2
2. Commission	6:8–10	1:5	2:3–7
3. Resistance/impediment to speech	6:5	1:6	
4. Divine assurance and	6:7	1:7–10; 17–19	1:8–3:3; 3:8–9
Preparation of the speaking mouth of the prophet	6:13	1:9–15	2:8–3:3

In each of the above, a commanding divine presence is felt, and the prophet recoils in fear and expresses inability to speak the word of God. In the case of Isaiah, a divine being purifies his "impure" mouth; in the case of Jeremiah, God says: "I will be with your mouth"; and, in the case of Ezekiel, there is the image of God placing His words into the mouth of the prophet in the form of a scroll. Physical imagery is thus used to communicate the prophet's role as spokesman of God. Similarly, when Moses claims to be "heavy of tongue and heavy of mouth," the issue seems less that of physical deformity than inability and inferiority before God. In the repetition of Moses' commission in Exodus 6, Moses further protests that he is of "uncircumcised lips" (vv. 12, 30); i.e., that he feels unable and impure—like Isaiah—to speak God's words.

What emerges from, and is expressed by, the foregoing literary pattern is the prophets' fear of chosenness by God; their terror of being confronted and elected for a task for which they feel unprepared and unworthy; and their realization that it is only by the grace of God's active presence that they are enabled to perform the task. This kind of dynamic bears a striking phenomenological resemblance to testimonies by artists who feel themselves in the grip of an overwhelming force at the moment of inspiration, mere vessels for bringing that "will" to formal realization.

On his way back to Egypt, after receiving the three additional signs enumerated in 4:1–9, and after the just-discussed recommission scene of 4:10–16, Moses is again addressed by God (4:21b–23):

Note all these signs [mofetim] which I have given you and perform them before Pharaoh. But I shall harden his heart and he will not release the people. Then you will say to

Pharaoh: "Thus says YHWH: Israel is my firstborn; therefore I say to you, release my son that he may worship me.
And if you refuse to release him, I shall surely kill your own
firstborn."

A new matter is introduced here. For the signs "which I have given
you" are now expressly intended for the Pharaoh as well, not just the
Israelites. Indeed, God says that if Pharaoh will not respond to the
signs and release the Israelites He, YHWH, will kill Pharaoh's own
firsborn son.

A similar double motivation for the "signs" appears in the extended plague-cycle of chapters 7–12:36. Thus, whereas it is stated in
7:3–5 that the signs to come are for the Egyptians who will, thereby,
"come to know" the power of YHWH, 10:1–2 states that they are *also*
intended for the Israelites: "in order that you will tell your sons and
daughters what I did in Egypt . . . and know that I am YHWH."

One may go further. Not only does Exodus 4:21b–23 serve to
anticipate the plagues forecast against the Egyptians in general terms, it
also has a *specific,* structural relation to them. It may thus be noted that
Exodus 4:21b–23, by virtue of its allusion to 4:1–9, includes three signs
plus a climactic fourth (the killing of the firstborn) to be enacted before
Pharaoh. This pattern of one triad plus a climax $(3+1)$ formally
anticipates the overall plague cycle (7:8–12:36) which is composed of
three triads plus a climax in which firstborn males are killed $(3+3+3+1)$.
The fact that two shorter versions of this pattern (two triads with
climactic fourth parts in which firstborn are killed) can also be found in
the historical liturgies of Psalms 78 (vv. 43–51) and 105 (vv. 27–36)
further strengthens the likelihood that Exod. 4:21b–23 is itself a varia-
tion on this structural form. While the climactic event in 4:21b-23 is
not explicitly called a sign, there can be little doubt as to its intent and
functions.

However, while there is a literary symmetry in the pattern of the
plagues forecast against the Egyptians $(3+1$ and $3+3+3+1)$, an asym-
metry apparently remains. The plagues in Exod. 7:8–12:36 are, as
noted, meant for the Egyptians *and* the Israelites (cf. 7:3–5 and 10:1–2),
whereas the triad-plus-climax structure of signs in 4:21b–23 does not
explicitly refer to the Israelites. There does not, then, seem to be a
fourth sign for them. If the death of the Egyptian firstborn in Exodus
12 is balanced by the life and liberation of the Israelites, no counterpoint seems to occur to offset the death of Pharaoh's firstborn son

mentioned in 4:23. Instead, a most unsettling event is described (vv. 24–26):

> And on the way, at a resting spot, YHWH encountered him and sought to kill him. Then Zipporah took a flint and cut off the foreskin of her son, and touched his penis, saying: "You are now a bridegroom of blood with YHWH." So he released him, and she said: "You are a bridegroom of blood through the circumcision."

This text is heavy with mystery and has confused generations of interpreters—for the context and various pronominal references are indeterminate. All that seems clear, at the most basic level, is that Moses was attacked by God on his return to Egypt. On the basis of the literary-structural remarks just offered, however, a symbolical understanding may now be offered. Just as 4:23 anticipates the death of the Egyptians through the figure of Pharaoh's firstborn, so do verses 24–26 anticipate the redemption of the Israelites, God's own firstborn (cf. v. 23), by focusing on the salvation and protection effected for Moses by the blood of his own son's circumcision. Moses and his firstborn thus counterpoint Pharaoh and his firstborn. Since this episode regarding Moses and his son *immediately follows* verses 21–23 and its pattern of triad-plus-climax, a corresponding 3 + 1 structure of signs also seems to obtain for the Israelites (i.e., 4:1–9, 24–26).

These literary-structural considerations may be complemented by a focus on 4:24–26 from the viewpoint of Moses' spiritual biography—for his life was not simply symbolic of national destiny, but was private and individual on its own terms. The narrative of Moses in Midian, 3:1–4:23, makes it clear that he is beset by doubts and ambivalences as regards his prophetic task. Perhaps due to the confusing and disrupting events of his childhood, Moses finds it initially difficult to trust a god who says He would "be as He would be." Now, at this most decisive moment in his life, when he gathers his strength to submit himself fully to God as a faithful messenger, Moses is tested in his resolve, in his capacity to acknowledge that He who referred to Himself as *'eheyeh,* "I shall be," is the same One whether He promises life and redemption or causes death and destruction. A true messenger, one faithful to his task, would have to know this truth and not resist it.

At all events, the narrator has undoubtedly transformed an ancient, even demonic, literary fragment in order to provide a dramatic externalization of an interior moment in Moses' spiritual life. Moses, who feels himself attacked by this life-promising God, is helped through his crises by his wife Zipporah, who turns his attention to his son and the future generation which his mission will ultimately benefit. Following this event Moses arrives in Egypt and displays the three signs given him to the Israelite elders (4:27–30), who immediately "trust" God's promise (4:31). The signs to Pharaoh and the Egyptians have yet to be given.

Before considering how Exodus 1–4 foreshadows Exodus 5–19, a brief clarification is due concerning the decision to limit the opening textual unit to the end of chapter 4. That this delimitation is not at all self-evident is easily confirmed by the fact that the breakdown of the various narrative subunits from Exod. 4:18 on are not clearly marked. The particular relationship of Exodus 5 to its textual environment is representative of the difficulties involved, and of direct pertinence to our present concern: Is Exodus 5 to be included with 4:18–6:1, as part of the return to Egypt (even though the signs of chapter 4 are nowhere mentioned when Moses and Aaron go before Pharaoh), or does it begin a new narrative sequence?

To answer this question several considerations are determinative, to my mind. First, the scene shifts back to Egypt only in Exodus 5, to which the preceding chapter is both a transition and an anticipation of tasks to be done. Second, there are many verbal and thematic echoes between Exodus 5 and the mise-en-scène of the Israelite servitude in Egypt in Exodus 1 (see discussion below), thus suggesting a renewed— though altogether new—stage in the drama of oppression and redemption. And third, it is precisely the failure of Moses before Pharaoh (chap. 5), together with Moses' sense of the countervailing effect of the revealed name (v. 23), which provide the motivation and apologia for the recommission scene in 6:22ff. Accordingly, the common tendency to separate Exodus 5 from what follows would appear to snap a deliberate narrative web (particularly compare 5:23 with 6:2–3).

Thus both because of its distinctions from chapter 4, and its links with chapter 6, Exodus 5 would seem to begin a new narrative phase. In it Moses and Aaron appear before Pharaoh in Egypt with the divine name and demand. To be sure, such an analytic estimation, based as it is on literary-typological considerations, is a meta-analysis arising from the *received* narrative tradition. For from the viewpoint of the distinguishable sources or traditions which comprise the narrative, Exod. 6:2ff. is linguistically distinct from—and even thematically contradictory to—chapter 5. But one may not doubt that these and many

other compositional problems facing the reader of the Exodus Cycle
are conditioned by a double concern of the final arranger-composer: to
both preserve diverse traditions (e.g., the two commission traditions
noted earlier) *and* to transform them into one continuous narrative. It
is, in fact, the suggestion of the following analysis that it was precisely
in the process of weaving together a continuous narrative from multi-
ple oral and literary traditions that the final arranger-composer stylized his materials typologically, so that the opening narrative (in Exodus
1–4) linguistically and thematically foreshadows or balances that which
follows (in Exodus 5–19).

Some of the links between the opening chapters of the Book of
Exodus and their sequel have already been intimated. Here, now,
follows a fuller explication of interrelations which obtain between the
opening unit of the Book of Exodus (part 1, chapters 1–4) and its
successor (part 2, chapters 5–19).

1. In Exod. 1:8–14 (part 1), the toil of the Israelites is levied by
Pharaoh because they have become numerous (*rav*, v. 7). When Moses
and Aaron later go to the Pharaoh to request the release of the Israelites
(5:5–19, part 2), he increases their toil because they have become even
more numerous (*rabbim*, v. 5). That Pharaoh is a new one, who has
ascended during Moses' absence in the Midianite wilderness (2:23).
The new unit (chap. 5) thus begins with a decree imposed by the (new)
Pharaoh, even as did the first (1:8–11).

2. In part 1, a second method is employed to curb the growth of
the Israelites: infanticide of male firstborn. Their babies are to be
drowned in the sea (Exod. 1:22); but Moses is saved (2:1–6). In part 2,
the Egyptians are drowned in the sea, while all Israel is saved (chaps.
14–15).

3. The first commission of Moses (part 1) occurs at the *sneh*-bush
(2:3), adjacent to a "mountain of God" (v. 1). Later (part 2), after the
Exodus, all Israel stands at *Sinai,* a "mountain of God" (Exod. 24:13).
The link is structural and linguistic.

4. In 3:6–11 and 4:10–17 (part 1) Moses is commissioned and complains of his inability to speak—of being "heavy of tongue." His
brother Aaron is thereupon designated his spokesman. As part of the
commission, God reveals Himself as God of the fathers (3:6, 16), refers
to the covenant-promise (3:7–9, 17–20), and states that the God of the
fathers is known as EHYeH (v. 14). These several features are replicated
in part 2: during the course of the succeeding events, God reveals
Himself to Moses as El Shaddai, God of the fathers (6:2), refers to the

covenant-promise (vv. 4–8), and reveals His name: YHWH. Moses, in turn, complains that he is of "uncircumcised lips" (6:12, 30). As with the previous phrase "heavy of tongue," this phrase equally refers to Moses' own sense of incompetence; and, as in part 1 (4:14–17), Aaron is again designated Moses' substitute (7:1–2). This second tradition of the commission serves to recommit Moses to his task and, as Greenberg has plausibly suggested, to stress the divine name YHWH and to introduce the central theme-idea of the second part: that Egyptians and Israelites alike must come to see that He is God.

5. In part 1, God gives Moses three signs, plus a fourth (4:1–9, 24–26), so that the Israelites will trust him (4:5, 8, 9). The first three signs are intended also for the Egyptians, while the killing of the firstborn is a sign directed to Pharaoh alone (4:21–23). These traditions appear in part 2 in expanded form. They reappear as ten plagues, or signs, taking the form 3 + 3 + 3 + 1. Strikingly, this triple literary triad was already detected in early Rabbinic times, as is evidenced by Rabbi Judah bar Ilai's Hebrew acronym for the plagues, memorialized in the Passover Haggadda: *DeTZaKH,'ADaSH,Be'AHaV*.

6. The fourth sign of the first sequence (Exodus 4), and the tenth sign of the second (chapt. 11–12), each involve the killing of firstborn Egyptians, in contrast to the redemption of Israelites, the firstborn of God. The protecting power of blood benefits the Israelites in each case. In part 2, the Israelites are protected by blood during the night of the paschal feast—when all the firstborn Egyptian males were killed (12:7–13). In Exod. 4:24–26 (part 1), Moses is protected by the circumcision blood of his firstborn. Early recognition of the thematic connection between Exod. 4:24–26, dealing with the apotropeic, or protective power of the blood of circumcision, and Exod. 12:13 where a similar power of blood recurs, can be found in the ancient Palestinian Targum traditions and the medieval Bible commentary by Rabbi Abraham ibn Ezra.

7. When Moses first showed the signs to the Israelites (4:27ff.), the nation "trusted" (*vayya'amen*, v. 31), even as all the Israelites later "trusted" (*vayya'aminu,* 14:31) in God and His servant Moses after the final manifestation of power against the Egyptians.

8. And finally, the encounter between Moses and God in 3:1ff. occurs at the mountain of God-Elohim, by a *sneh*-bush. The original confirmation sign by God to Moses at the commission was that after the exodus the people would "worship Elohim at this mountain" (v. 12). The geographical reference "at this mountain" is, according to

many scholars, the *sneh*-bush referred to in verses 1-4. And indeed, after the exodus the people do go to a mountain called "mountain of Elohim" (24:13), also called *Sinai* (19:11, 20), located in the wilderness of Sin (19:1-2). The thematic link between the units is thus further underscored by the acoustical similarity of *sneh*/Sinai.

The function of the foreshadowing in part 1 is to interconnect the saga-cycle by means of recurrent images and language. While these interrelations are inobtrusively textured into the overall cycle, their analysis enhances our appreciation of the narrative art of Exodus 1-19 and reveals the inner-textual issues which occupied its author's imagination. The various dimensions of the foreshadowing cycle can be recapitulated and further expanded through the following detailed chart.

Exodus 1-4	*Exodus 5-19*
1. The Egyptians embitter the Israelites' labor (*sivlotam*) through mortar and (*livenim*) bricks; 1:11-14.	After Moses and Aaron appear before Pharoah their labor (*sivlotam*) is made difficult through straw and bricks (*livenim*); 5:4ff.
2. For they have multiplied (*va-yirbu*); 1:7, cf. 9:12.	For, Pharoah says, "Indeed, the people are many" (*rabbim*); 5:5.
3. Pharoah commands that every Israelite male be thrown into the Nile; 1:22.	At the Exodus, "God threw the chariots of Pharoah and his retinue into the sea"; 14:15-15:19.
4. But Moses is saved; 2:1ff.	But the Israelites are saved; 14:15-15:19.
5. YHWH appears to Moses at the *sneh,* the mountain of God; 3:1-2.	YHWH appears to Moses (6:2ff.), and all Israelites at *Sinai,* the mountain of God; 19:1ff.
6. The God of the fathers hears the cry of His people and prepares to bring them to Canaan, the Promised Land 3:6-8.	The God of the fathers hears the wail of His people and remembers His promise to bring them to Canaan; 6:4-8.
7. At his commission, Moses is fearful (3:11) and complains that he is "heavy of mouth and tongue," 4:10, so God says: "Aaron will be to you as a mouth, and you will be to him as an Elohim," 4:14-16.	At his commission, Moses is fearful and complains that he is of "uncircumcised lips," 6:12, 30, so God says: "See I have appointed you Elohim to Pharoah, and your brother, Aaron, will be your prophet," 7:1.

8. YHWH instructs the Israelites, through Moses, to take (stem: *sha'al*) silver, etc. from the Egyptians and to despoil (stem: *natzal*) them at the Exodus: 3:21–22.	"And the Israelites did according to Moses' instructions" and took all (stem: *sha'al*) silver utensils from Egypt, so that they despoiled (stem: *natzal*) the Egyptians; 12:35–36.
9. 3+1 signs are given for the Israelites (and also the Egyptians); 4:22ff.	9+1 signs occur for the Egyptians (and also the Israelites); 7–11.
10. The fourth sign to Pharoah involves the death of his firstborn; 4:23.	The tenth sign to Pharoah involves the death of Egyptian firstborn; 11:1ff.
11. The apotropeic power of blood deflects divine wrath; 4:24ff.	The apotropeic power of blood deflects divine destruction; 12:7ff.
12. The signs are displayed before the nation . . . and it believed (*vayya'amen*); 4:31.	At the sea "all Israel saw the mighty hand and believed (*vayya'minu*) in YHWH"; 14:31.

We began this [essay] . . . by indicating several anticipatory links between the Book of Genesis and the Book of Exodus. It may be appropriate to close with another. The exodus event so dominated Israelite theological and historiographical imagination that it affected even the formulation of the Abrahamic traditions. A hint in this direction occurs at the very beginning of the Patriarchal Cycle, in Gen. 12:10–20. Immediately after his entrance into the land, Abram *migrates* to *Egypt* because of famine (*ra'av*) and sojourns (stem: *gwr*) there. After an episode in which he introduced his wife, Sarah, as his sister—thereby setting the stage for Pharaoh's amorous advances—YHWH brings plagues (stem: *naga'*) against Pharaoh and his household (v. 17). In response, the Pharaoh sends (stem: *shalah*) him out of Egypt, where he has accumulated great wealth (v. 16; 13:1). Both the narrative and language of Gen. 12:10–20 are clearly reminiscent of the Exodus Cycle, where *shalah* and *gwr* are common terms, and *naga'* is used regarding a plague in 11:1.

Exodus: The Definitive Deliverance

Northrop Frye

We referred earlier, [in *The Great Code*] to the structure of the Book of Judges, in which a series of stories of traditional tribal heroes is set within a repeating *mythos* of the apostasy and restoration of Israel. This gives us a narrative structure that is roughly U-shaped, the apostasy being followed by a descent into disaster and bondage, which in turn is followed by repentance, then by a rise through deliverance to a point more or less on the level from which the descent began. This U-shaped pattern, approximate as it is, recurs in literature as the standard shape of comedy, where a series of misfortunes and misunderstandings brings the action to a threateningly low point, after which some fortunate twist in the plot sends the conclusion up to a happy ending. The entire Bible, viewed as a "divine comedy," is contained within a U-shaped story of this sort, one in which man, as explained, loses the tree and water of life at the beginning of Genesis and gets them back at the end of Revelation. In between, the story of Israel is told as a series of declines into the power of heathen kingdoms, Egypt, Philistia, Babylon, Syria, Rome, each followed by a rise into a brief moment of relative independence. The same U-narrative is found outside the historical sections also, in the account of the disasters and restoration of Job and in Jesus' parable of the prodigal son. This last, incidentally, is the only version in which the redemption takes place as the result of a voluntary decision on the part of the protagonist (Luke 15:18).

It would be confusing to summarize all the falls and rises of the

From *The Great Code: The Bible and Literature.* © 1982 by Northrop Frye. Harcourt Brace Jovanovich, 1982.

biblical history at once. In honor of the days of creation, let us select six, with a seventh forming at the end of time. The first fall, naturally, is that of Adam from Eden, where Adam goes into a wilderness that modulates to the heathen cities founded by the family of Cain. Passing over the story of Noah, which adds the sea to the images of disaster, the first rise is that of Abraham, called out of the city of Ur in Mesopotamia to a Promised Land in the west. This introduces the pastoral era of the patriarchs, and ends at the end of Genesis, with Israel in Egypt. This situation again changes to an oppressive and threatening servitude; Israel again passes through a sea and a wilderness, and under Moses and Joshua reaches its promised land again, a smaller territory where the main images are agricultural. There succeed the invaders in the Book of Judges, of whom the most formidable where the Philistines, probably a Greek-speaking people from Crete (if that is the "Caphtor" of Amos 9:7) who gave their name to Palestine. They held the mastery of Israel after the defeat and death of Saul and his son Jonathan. The third rise begins with David and continues with Solomon, where the imagery is urban, concerned with cities and buildings. After Solomon, however, another disaster begins with the splitting of the kingdom. The northern kingdom was destroyed by Assyria in 722 B.C.; the southern kingdom of Judah had a reprieve until after Assyria was destroyed in its turn (Nah. 2:3ff.); but with the capture of Jerusalem by Nebuchadnezzar in 586 the Babylonian captivity began.

The fourth rise in the fortunes of the Israelites, now the Jews, begins with the permission—perhaps the encouragement—given the Jewish captives in Babylon by Cyrus of Persia to return and rebuild their temple. Two returns are prominently featured in the Old Testament, and there were probably more, but symbolically we need only one. Some flickering hopes of a restored Israel clustered around the chief figure of the first return, Zerubbabel of the line of David. After several changes of masters, the next dramatic descent was caused by the savage persecution of the non-Hellenized Jews by Antiochus Epiphanes of the Seleucian empire, which provoked the rebellion of the Maccabees, five brothers of a priestly family who finally gained independence for Judea and established a royal dynasty. This lasted until the Roman legions under Pompey rolled over the country in 63 B.C., and began the Roman domination that lasts throughout the New Testament period. At this point Jewish and Christian views of the sixth deliverance of Israel diverge. For Christianity, Jesus achieved a definitive deliverance for all mankind with his revelation that the ideal kingdom of Israel was a spiritual kingdom. For Judaism, the expulsion from their homeland by the edict of Hadrian in 135 A.D. began a renewed exile which in many respects still endures.

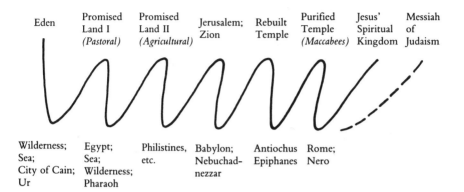

This is a sequence of *mythoi,* only indirectly of historical events, and our first step is to realize that all the high points and all the low points are metaphorically related to one another. That is, the garden of Eden, the Promised Land, Jerusalem, and Mount Zion are interchangeable synonyms for the home of the soul, and in Christian imagery they are all identical, in their "spiritual" form (which we remember means metaphorically, whatever else it may also mean), with the kingdom of God spoken of by Jesus. Similarly, Egypt, Babylon, and Rome are all spiritually the same place, and the Pharaoh of the Exodus, Nebuchadnezzar, Antiochus Epiphanes, and Nero are spiritually the same person. And the deliverers of Israel—Abraham, Moses and Joshua, the judges, David, and Solomon—are all prototypes of the Messiah or final deliverer.

Of all the upward movements on our chart, the primary and model form is the deliverance from Egypt, and the creation of the nation of Israel that formed part of this deliverance. As the various declines of Israel through apostasy and the like are not acts so much as failures to act, it is only the rises and restorations that are real events, and as the Exodus is the definitive deliverance and the type of all the rest, we may say that mythically the Exodus is the only thing that really happens in the Old Testament. On the same principle the resurrection of Christ, around which the New Testament revolves, must be, from the New Testament's point of view, the antitype of the Exodus. The life of Christ as presented in the Gospels becomes less puzzling when we realize that it is being presented in this form.

Like that of many gods and heroes, the birth of Jesus is a threatened birth: Herod orders a massacre of infants in Bethlehem from which Jesus alone escapes. Moses similarly escapes from an attempt to destroy Hebrew children, as they in turn escape later from a slaughter of Egyptian firstborn. The infant Jesus is taken down into Egypt by Joseph and Mary, and his return from there, Matthew (2:15) says, fulfills the prophecy of Hosea (11:1) "I called my son out of Egypt," where the reference is quite explicitly to Israel. The names Mary and Joseph recall the Miriam who was the sister of Moses and the Joseph who led the family of Israel into Egypt. The third Sura of the Koran appears to be identifying Miriam and Mary; Christian commentators on the Koran naturally say that this is ridiculous, but from the purely typological point of view from which the Koran is speaking, the identification makes good sense.

Moses organizes the twelve tribes of Israel; Jesus gathers twelve disciples. Israel crosses the Red Sea and achieves its identity as a nation on the other side; Jesus is baptized in the Jordan and is recognized as the Son of God. The baptism is the point at which Mark and John begin, the infancy stories of Matthew and Luke being probably later material. Israel wanders forty years in the wilderness; Jesus, forty days. Miraculous food is provided for Israel and by Jesus for those gathered around him (see John 6:49–50). The law is given from Mount Sinai and the gospel preached in the Sermon on the Mount. A brazen serpent is placed on a pole by Moses as preservation against the fatal bites of "fiery serpents" (Num. 21:9); this brazen serpent was accepted by Jesus as a type of his crucifixion (John 3:14), with an underlying association between the lethal serpents and the serpent of Eden. Moses dies just outside the Promised Land, which in Christian typology signifies the inability of the law alone to redeem man, and the Promised Land is conquered by Joshua. The hidden link here is that Jesus and Joshua are the same word, hence when the Virgin Mary is told to call her child Jesus or Joshua, the typological meaning is that the reign of the law is over, and the assault on the Promised Land has begun (Matt. 1:21).

This is the longer version of the parallel: the shorter one is still more important typologically. The core of the Exodus story is the interval between the last plague and the crossing of the Red Sea, and it contains three main events. First is the destruction of the Egyptian firstborn by a destroying angel, which the Israelites escaped by smearing the blood of a lamb on their doorposts. This is the archetype of the Passover festival. Second is the drowning of the Egyptian army in the Red Sea, and third is the crossing of the Red Sea by the Israelites to the desert beyond. The life of Christ also has a longer version in the upper air, so to speak, in which he comes "down" from heaven, metaphorically the sky ("descendit de coelis," as the Creed says), to be born on the earth, goes through his ministry on the earth, and goes back into the sky with the Ascension. This movement is repeated on a lower level in the Passion, where Jesus dies on the cross on Good Friday, is buried, descends to the lower world during what from the Christian point of view was the last Sabbath, and returns to the surface of the earth in the Resurrection on Easter Sunday morning.

It follows that the crossing of the Red Sea, leaving the Egyptians still in it, is the type, not merely of Jesus' baptism in the long version, but of the Resurrection in the short one. Hence the imagery of such Easter hymns as this fourth-century one of St. Ambrose:

> For these are our paschal solemnities, in which the very lamb is slain, by whose blood the doorposts of the faithful are made holy.
>
> This is the night in which thou, Lord, didst first lead our fathers, the children of Israel, out of Egypt and make them cross the Red Sea on dry foot.
>
> This is the night in which Christ broke the bonds of death and rose again as a victor from hell.
>
> O truly blessed night, which alone was worthy of knowing the time and the hour at which Christ rose from the dead!

The Gospels could hardly be more careful than they are to synchronize the Crucifixion with the feast of the Passover, to make it utterly clear that the Passion, as they saw it, was the antitype of the Passover sacrifice.

The contrast with the birth date of Jesus is curious. There is no evidence in the New Testament about the time of year at which he was born, and in celebrating Christmas the Church was apparently content to take over the winter solstice festival from other religions. The most important event in the Mithraic ritual calendar was the birthday of the sun, celebrated on December 25. In Christian typology too Christ was a rising "sun of righteousness" (Mal. 4:2), and Milton's *Nativity Ode* will serve as an example of hundreds of poems that testify to the appropriateness of the winter solstice date. There was perhaps some influence too from Hanukkah, the Jewish feast of the Dedication of the Temple, observed by Jesus when he was in Jerusalem (John 10:22). This was not a winter solstice festival, but it does feature lights and celebrates the birth of a new and purified temple on the anniversary of its pollution by Antiochus Epiphanes (2 Macc. 10:5). This makes it a type of the birth of Christ in the physical body of Adam (John 2:19). Hanukkah was celebrated on the twenty-fifth of Chislev, which is not the twenty-fifth of December, but the coincidence of numbers is interesting.

Mythical and typological thinking are not rational thinking, and we have to get used to conceptions that do not follow ordinary distinctions of categories and are, so to speak, liquid rather than solid (not gaseous: they tend to keep their volume if not their form). In the later commentary on the Exodus story known as the Book of Wisdom we read:

> For while peaceful silence enwrapped all things, and night in her own swiftness was in mid course, thine all-powerful Word leaped from heaven out of the royal throne.
>
> (18:14f.)

This refers, in its own context, to something totally different from the birth of Christ, but it is the only type we have of the birth story recorded in Luke, which has Jesus born at midnight. Similarly, in the Church calendar the forty days of wilderness wandering by Jesus are commemorated in Lent, which is immediately followed by Good Friday and Easter, although in the Gospels the whole ministry of Jesus intervened. T. S. Eliot's "Ash-Wednesday" is based on a structure of parallels between the Church calendar, Dante's *Purgatorio,* and various elements in the Bible:

	OLD TESTAMENT	NEW TESTAMENT	DANTE	CHURCH CALENDAR
1	Promised Land	Resurrection	Eden	Easter
2	Wilderness Wandering	Wilderness Wandering	Purgatory	Lent
3	Red Sea	Baptism (Jordan)	Sea	(Ash Wednesday)

The Christian Bible, considered as a narrative, has for its hero the Messiah, who emerges, as frequently happens in romances, with his own name and identity only near the end. Being the Word of God that spoke all things into being, he is the creator of Genesis, and the secret presence in Old Testament history—the rock that followed the Israelites with water, as Paul says in a passage (1 Cor. 10:4) already referred to. He enters the physical world at his Incarnation, achieves his conquest of death and hell in the lower world after his death on the cross, and, according to later legend, "harrows hell," extracting from limbo the souls destined to be saved, from Adam and Eve through to John the Baptist. Then, as noted, he reappears in the physical world at his Resurrection and goes back into the sky with Ascension. Thus:

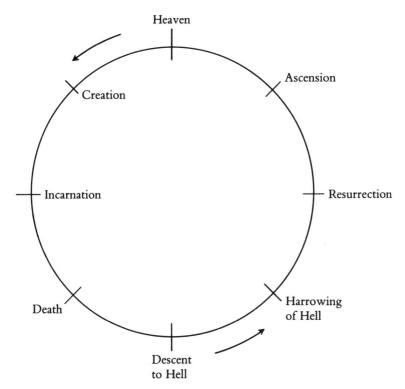

There is a considerable foreshortening of time in the thousands of years between the first two intervals and the "three days and three nights" in the lower world—two nights and one day, according to our reckoning. We also see the working of a principle we have met before: that what fills out a scheme and is not mentioned, or is only doubtfully referred to, in the Bible is very apt to be supplied by later legend. The New Testament evidence for the descent into hell is weak, and the "harrowing of hell," though extremely popular in the Middle Ages, is purely apocryphal, deriving from a work known as the Gospel of Nicodemus or the Acts of Pilate.

It may seem inconsistent to show the messianic quest as a cycle when the anticyclical bias of the Bible has been so stressed, but this is one more example of the fact that every apocalyptic image has a demonic parody or contrast, and vice versa. The quest of Christ can be thought of as a cycle, because, however important for man, it involved no essential change in the divine nature itself. The nearest suggestion of such a change is the liturgical metaphor that places Christ in the middle of the Trinity before his quest and on the right after it. There is also a demonic cycle caused, not by an impersonal fate, but by the fate deliberately generated out of the pride and folly of ambitious conquerors. If we look back at our manic-depressive chart, we find that the sequence of U's can also be seen as a sequence of rises and falls of heathen kingdoms, each an inverted U, which differs from a cyclical movement only in the fact that at each turn of the wheel the empire has a different name: Egypt, Assyria, Babylon, Persia, Macedonia, Syria, Rome. The inverted U is the typical shape of tragedy, as its opposite is of comedy: it rises to a point of "peripety" or reversal of action, then plunges downward to a "catastrophe," a word which contains the figure of "turning down." The Bible does not however think of this movement as tragic but simply as ironic: it concentrates on the final collapse and minimizes or ignores the heroic element in the historical achievements that preceded it.

In the Exodus-Gospel parallel we saw Jesus as following the rising movement of the redemption of Israel, of which the Exodus is the chief prototype. But the Incarnation was a voluntary descent into a lower world repeating the creation of Adam, hence Paul characterizes Jesus as a second Adam (1 Cor. 15:45). There is in Genesis a type of such a descent, not wholly voluntary, in the story of Joseph, whose "coat of many colors" suggests fertility-god imagery, and who, like Burns's John Barleycorn, is thrown into a pit. The pit modulates to Egypt, where, after shaking off the attachment to this lower world represented by Potiphar's wife, he becomes chief adviser to the Pharaoh through his skill in interpreting dreams. A related story is told of Daniel, who performs a similar service for Nebuchadnezzar and also undergoes tests of faith. Both dreams have to do with historical cycles.

Pharaoh's is of a seven-year cycle of alternating plenty and famine, connected with the great importance of seven-year cycles in the Near East that is also reflected in the "jubilee" regulations in Leviticus 25. Nebuchadnezzar's is of a statue representing a sequence of world empires, beginning with his own, which are destroyed by a stone rolling downhill, representing in turn the messianic kingdom that puts an end to all cycles of power in history.

The House of Bondage: Slaves in Egypt

Michael Walzer

I

The strength of Exodus history lies in its end, the divine promise. It is also true, of course, that the significance and value of the end is given by the beginning. Canaan is a promised land because Egypt is a house of bondage. Beginning and end stand in a necessary relation. The Exodus is not a lucky escape from misfortune. Rather, the misfortune has a moral character, and the escape has a world-historical meaning. Egypt is not just left behind; it is rejected; it is judged and condemned. The crucial terms of that judgment are *oppression* and *corruption,* and I shall examine each of these in turn. But I must stress first that the judgment is conceivable only because of the promise; its moral force requires the idea, at least, of a life that is neither oppressive nor corrupt. God's promise generates a sense of possibility (it would be rash, given the fearfulness of the Israelite slaves, to say that it generates a sense of confidence): the world is not all Egypt. Without that sense of possibility, oppression would be experienced as an inescapable condition, a matter of personal or collective bad luck, a stroke of fate. There are indeed religious standpoints from which one can judge the world as a whole and find it oppressive and corrupt—Satan's world. But Pharaoh is not Satan, and the biblical judgment is not of that sort. Its moral quality depends upon the existence of alternative possibilities here and now. Anger and hope, not resignation, are the appropriate responses to the Egyptian house of bondage.

From *Exodus and Revolution.* © 1985 by Basic Books, Inc.

The point can be made more forcefully by way of a comparison. Euripides' *Women of Troy* provides a useful contrast with the Exodus story, for it describes a "going out" that leads to slavery rather than to freedom. Thus, Hecabe, at the end of the play:

> Come, trembling aged feet,
> You must not fail me now.
> There your way lies: forward into slavery!

The women have been abandoned by the gods of their city. For them there is no promise. "I have not even the common human blessing of hope," says Andromache; "I cannot delude myself with the pleasant dream of . . . happiness in the future." Without illusion, the women steadfastly confront (and bewail) their destiny. Slavery is the natural consequence of defeat; the Greeks exult, the women weep: everyone behaves as expected.

Euripides makes no moral judgment; at least, he makes no judgment of the slavery into which the woman are led. The feeling that he means to evoke is pity, not anger or indignation. We are, perhaps, invited to be angry at particular acts of cruelty—the murders of Hecabe's daughter and of Andromache's (and Hector's) son. But we are meant above all to pity the women, particularly the noble women, for whom slavery is an agony of the soul. In aristocratic eyes, the loss of freedom is "the height of disgrace," as a modern historian [Joseph Vogt] writes, and also, mixing his metaphors, "a sudden fall into the void." Euripides wants to remind his contemporaries, who have just enslaved the women of Melos, of how sudden such falls can be. Bondage is certainly oppressive in his portrayal, but it is not unjust. It is oppressive like a hot and humid summer day—infinitely worse, of course, but like that nonetheless. Slavery, to quote the dictionary now, "lies heavy on, weighs down, crushes the feelings, mind, spirits." This is the argument of the play; what Euripides has written is the long lament of the Trojan women.

The language of Exodus is sometimes similar in tone. Slavery is described in the first chapters of the book as an "affliction," a "burden," a "sorrow." Clearly, the Israelites found slavery oppressive, just as the Greeks did. But the Greeks also found war and disease, sieges and fevers oppressive; they consistently used the word *piezein,* derived (like the Hebrew *lachatz*) from a root meaning "to press down," in a nonmoral sense. In the literature of fifth- and fourth-century Athens (B.C.E.), so far as I can tell, the word is standardly used in the passive voice and always with an impersonal subject: "oppressed by war," "oppressed by fever." By contrast, biblical usage is active and personal. It is crucial to the Exodus story and explicit in the text that Pharaoh and his taskmasters oppressed the children of Israel. "Behold," God says to Moses, "I have seen the oppression wherewith the Egyptians oppress them" (Exod. 3:9). The dictionary puts the two definitions, impersonal and personal, passive and active, side by side, but it is this second meaning that has been so important in the political history of the West: "to keep under by tyrannical exercise of power, to burden . . . with cruel or unjust impositions or restraints."

Perhaps I should be more careful. Pharaoh is never explicitly called a tyrant in the Book of Exodus, though he is known ever after in Jewish literature as the first of the tyrants. The warnings about the dangers of kingship in Deuteronomy 17 and 1 Samuel 8 obviously look back to Pharaoh's Egypt. Nor is the oppression of the Israelites actually called unjust (it is called cruel). One of the Hebrew words sometimes translated as oppression ('ani, also, and better, translated as "affliction") more nearly expresses misery and pain than wrongful injury. And yet the wrongfulness of Israel's bondage is surely the argument of the text. So the text has been read, at any rate, from the earliest times. Thus, it is commonly said that when Moses killed the Egyptian taskmaster, he acted rightly, punishing a wrongdoer. Some of the rabbis worried that the punishment was excessive, since the taskmaster had not killed, but only beaten, the Israelite slave; but even they agreed that Moses' anger was righteous. It is a good thing to stand against oppression. Much of the moral code of the Torah is explained and defended in opposition to Egyptian cruelty. The Israelites are commanded to act justly, which is to say, not as the Egyptians acted; and the motive of their action is to be the memory of the injustice their ancestors suffered in Egypt and which they suffer again, through the remembering, in the Egypt of their minds.

The new regime is defined by contrast with the old. Not only *this* new regime, the commonwealth founded by Moses: in an important sense, the language of revolutionary politics generally (and of religious messianism, too) is first developed and deployed here. Oppression takes on the moral significance it has had in the Judeo-Christian world ever since. And the possibility of deliverance and redemption is decisively broached. The word "redemption" derives, in Hebrew as in English, from a legal term meaning "to buy back"—in this case, the freedom of a slave. The Hebrew noun translated as "deliverance" comes from the verb "to go out." But it is only if one goes out from

Egypt (not, say, from Troy) that one is delivered. In England in the 1640s, "deliverance" played roughly the same role as "liberation" plays today: the two words are closely related, and like "redemption" they take their larger meanings from the experience of slavery. It may be the case that other experiences of slavery have generated similar meanings. When the Spartan helots, for example, whose condition in some ways resembled that of Israel in Egypt, rebelled against their masters, we can be certain that they aimed to set themselves free. But we don't know what they made of their freedom once they had won it, with Theban help, in 371 B.C.E. Did they "remember" their bondage when they celebrated their deliverance? Did they shape a new politics in the light of that memory? Probably they did not, for slavery was a degraded and shameful condition in ancient Greece, and former slaves tried most often to escape their past, to forget rather than to remember. In any case, we have no account of the helot idea of deliverance; nor did that idea, whatever it was, have any further influence; whereas it is possible to trace a continuous history from the Exodus to the radical politics of our own time.

II

I won't try to do that, however; I want to focus instead on what happened in Egypt. What was the nature of the oppression? Certainly, it wasn't slavery itself, at least, not chattel slavery. The Israelites were not bought and sold in Egypt; nor is slavery in this sense barred (though it is extensively regulated) in the legal code that comes out of the Exodus experience. We might better say that the Israelites were guests in Egypt, later on, guest workers, later on still, state slaves, subjected to a kind of *corvée*. Many Egyptians were similarly subject; that's why Egypt was called a "house of bondage" (literally: house of slaves). What features of the house of bondage do we highlight when we describe it as tyrannical? What specifically were its unjust impositions? Why did Egyptian bondage become the original and archetypal form of oppression?

The easiest modern reading of the first chapter of the Book of Exodus is social and economic in character; we are accustomed to think of oppression in those terms. Lincoln Steffens provides a nice example when he calls Moses a "loyal labor leader." A contemporary Latin American priest describes the suffering of the Israelites under four headings: repression, alienated work, humiliation, and enforced

birth control. That last phrase might refer to a midrashic story according to which the Egyptians worked their male slaves so hard and long
that they could not return to their wives at night but fell asleep,
exhausted, in their workplaces. Or it might refer—though the euphe-
mism would be a bit odd for a theologian of liberation—to Pharaoh's
order to the midwives to kill the newborn sons of the Israelites. This is
infanticide, not birth control; its purpose was to destroy the entire
people of Israel by destroying the male line, leaving a population of
women and girls to be dispersed as slaves among Egyptian households.
I won't say much more about this aspect of Pharaoh's policy. Among
Jews it has come to be seen as the first of a series of attempts on Jewish
peoplehood that culminates in the Nazi death camps. Indeed, the
Pharaoh of the oppression does sound oddly like a modern anti-
Semite, worrying (in Exod. 1:10) about the growing power of the
Israelites, who had prospered in Egypt, and their possible disloyalty:
"lest they join also unto our enemies." But it isn't the killing of the
sons that figures in the earliest discussions of the Exodus story in
Deuteronomy and the Prophets. Nor is the killing central to non-
Jewish understandings of Egyptian bondage—not, at least, until Cath-
olic priests began to take an interest in liberation. Nor does this part of
the story make the persistent longing of the Israelites to return to
Egypt easy to understand. One can, indeed, pine for one's oppressor,
but not for the murderer of one's children.

The central tradition focuses on the *corvée*, not on the attempted
genocide. "And they made their lives bitter with hard bondage, in
mortar, and in brick, and in all manner of service in the field; all their
service, wherein they made them serve, was with rigor" (Exod. 1:14).
The Hebrew word for "with rigor" is *be-farech*, and it occurs only one
other time in the Torah, in Leviticus 25, where the laws for the
treatment of Israelite slaves are laid down: "Thou shalt not rule over
[them] with rigor," that is, as the Egyptians did. Many years later
Maimonides effectively extended this protection to all slaves, and at
the same time he offered a definition of *be-farech*. Rigorous service, he
suggested, is service without the limits of time or purpose. Bondage
involves work without end; hence it is work that both exhausts and
degrades the slave. Writing in the sixteenth century, the author of the
Vindiciae takes a similar view: the tyrant, he says, "erects idle and
needless trophies to continually employ his tributaries, that they might
want leisure to think on other things, as Pharaoh did the Jews."
Because of what Pharaoh did, perhaps, biblical legislation sets a limit

on the term of enslavement—though a limit that applies only to Israelite slaves: "If thou buy an Hebrew servant, six years he shall serve: and in the seventh he shall go out free for nothing" (Exod. 21:2). We don't know if the limit was ever enforced, but it was not forgotten. The prophet Jeremiah blames the fall of Judea and the Babylonian exile on the failure of the people to "proclaim liberty" to enslaved brothers and neighbors after six years, as they had covenanted to do, he says, when God brought them up out of Egypt (34:8–23). It may be that the freedom of the seventh day—an easier matter—was more widely accepted than the freedom of the seventh year. In Deuteronomy, the reason given for the establishment of the Sabbath is "that thy manservant and thy maidservant may rest as well as thou . . . remember that thou wast a servant in the land of Egypt" (Deut. 5:14; see also Exod. 23:12). This commandment includes all slaves, not only Israelites but also "strangers." It is based, no doubt, on a certain view of physical and spiritual needs but also on the memory of the degraded character of "rigorous" slavery. Alienated work and humiliation do capture at least part of the oppressiveness of Egyptian bondage.

One might, alternatively, understand *be-farech* in the sense of physical cruelty. Here, too, the laws proclaimed immediately after the escape from Egypt, where the Israelites had been beaten and killed, seem designed to rule out Egyptian oppression: "And if a man smite his servant or his maid . . . and he die under his hand; he shall surely be punished" (Exod. 21:20). Slave-owners who kill their slaves are not "put to death," as in the case of ordinary murder (see 21:12), so this isn't quite what Ephraim Urbach calls it: the "absolute equality of slave and free man in all matters regarding the judicial safeguarding of their lives." Still, the safeguards established by the Exodus prohibitions have "no parallel in either Greek or Roman law." Moreover, if a slave suffered physical injury at the hands of his master, he was to be set free (21:26–27). Again, we don't know if these laws were enforced, or how consistently they were enforced, during different periods of Israel's history. But they are Exodus laws, and they presumably express the Israelite understanding of their own suffering in Egypt.

It was also part of the oppressiveness of Egyptian slavery that the Israelites were not, in their own view, legitimately slaves at all. They had not been captured in war, and they had never sold themselves into bondage. They were, as I have said, a guest people, and then they were guest workers. This was the injustice committed by the Egyptians, according to the philosopher Philo: they made slaves "of men who were not only free but guests [and] suppliants." An old legend, retold in the Midrash, has it that the Israelites were at first paid wages for their work on the store cities Pithom and Raamses. Then the wages were withheld, and they were simply forced to work. This experience—some dim memory of it or some story about it elaborated over the years—seems to lie behind the Deuteronomic law of wages:

> Thou shalt not oppress an hired servant that is poor and needy, whether he be of thy brethren or of thy strangers that are in thy land. . . . At his day thou shalt give him his hire, neither shall the sun go down upon it. [And then, after two more commandments:] For thou shalt remember that thou wast a bondsman in Egypt.
>
> (25:14–15, 18)

The law is given in the singular, but it is a crucial part of the experience of the Israelites in Egypt that they were not enslaved one by one, but all together. They were made "poor and needy" because they were strangers in the land. Dependent upon political protection, they found themselves helpless when protection was suddenly withdrawn. They were not the victims of the market but of the state, the absolute monarchy of the pharaohs. Hence, Samuel's warning to the elders of Israel against choosing a king, which is surely meant to recall the Exodus experience: "And he shall take . . . your goodliest young men . . . and put them to work . . . and ye shall be his servants" (1 Sam. 8:16–17). Under an absolute king, it might be said, the whole body of subjects are like strangers in Egypt.

Egyptian bondage was the bondage of a people to the arbitrary power of the state. Chattel slavery was conceivably preferable, for it was a condition governed by legal norms. In "the house of slaves," there were no norms. The Israelites were submitted to a bondage without limit—without rest, without recompense, without restraint, without a purpose that they might make their own. In Egypt, slavery was a kind of political rule. Of course, Pharaoh profited from the work of his Israelite slaves, but he did not enslave them for the sake of the profit. The slaves were exploited, as all slaves are, but it is more important in the biblical account that they were oppressed, that is, ruled with cruelty, ruled tyrannically. The Exodus tradition speaks against tyranny—and that is the way it figures, for example, in the preaching of Savonarola, in the pamphlets of John Milton, and in American revolutionary sermons attacking the "British Pharaoh."

The form of the tyranny, of course, was hard labor, and so the story invites, again, a social and economic translation. The neat line that Hannah Arendt draws, in her book on revolution, between the political question and the social question, between tyranny and misery, cannot be drawn here. The Exodus story seems to encompass both. In applications of the story, the people of Israel are readily compared to an oppressed class. A pamphlet by the Leveller John Lilburne, published in London in 1645, suggests that this sort of thing isn't only a modern reading or misreading of the text.

> But some will say, that our bondage is not yet so bad as that of Egypt was, for all the Jews were in great bondage under the Egyptians, and yet many of ours are exempted; unto that I yield, and do confess that few of our great and mighty men do either work the clay or make the bricks; but they lay either all or most part of the burden on the poor by heavy labor.

The Deuteronomic command about the "poor and needy" makes a similar point: like Lilburne's England, the promised land breeds its own oppressors—"*our* great and mighty men." One doesn't need Egyptians. But the biblical writers attempt no extended social reference. The only groups that the text knows are ethnic and political in character, and the Exodus is first of all an account of the oppression of such a group by a savage ruler in a foreign land. That's why the memory of the Exodus is more often invoked on behalf of aliens than on behalf of slaves: "Thou shalt not oppress a stranger: for ye know the heart [*nefesh:* "spirit" or "feelings"] of a stranger, seeing ye were strangers in the land of Egypt" (Exod. 23:9). It is easy to understand why the Exodus story appealed so much to African slaves in the American South. Though these were chattel slaves, they were also aware of themselves as a separate people, strangers in a strange land, who shared a common fate. Egyptian bondage is paradigmatic for abolitionist politics, and for radical politics generally, because of its collective character. It invites a collective response—not manumission, the common goal of Greek and Roman slaves, but liberation.

We can think of the Exodus as an example of what is today called "national liberation." The people as a whole are enslaved, and then the people as a whole are delivered. At the same time, however, the uses of the story in Israel's own history—first in legislation and then in prophecy—suggest that the Egyptian model reaches to every sort of oppression and to every sort of liberation. Perhaps the crucial point is the linking of oppression and state power: "the oppression in Egypt," as Croatto says, "is of a *political* order . . . [it is] exercised from the seat of political power." Hence the escape from bondage is also the defeat of a tyrant—and the escape is only possible because of the defeat. Tyranny is symbolized by Pharaoh's horses and chariots, the core of his army and the source of his power (the symbolism recurs throughout the Bible). The overlord of the house of slaves is also an arrogant warlord, and so he is presented in the song of triumph that the Israelites sing on the far side of the Red Sea:

> The enemy said, I will pursue, I will overtake, I will divide
> the spoil, my lust shall be satisfied upon them; I will draw
> my sword, my hand shall destroy them.
>
> (Exod. 15:9)

But God is a greater warrior, and the tyrant is defeated: "the horse and his rider hath he thrown into the sea." This was the moment of liberation. Benjamin Franklin's proposal for the Great Seal captures the political sense of the Exodus text. Franklin went beyond the text, however, with his proposed inscription: "Resistance to tyrants is obedience to God." In Exodus history, . . . the Israelites do not themselves fight against Pharaoh. It is God alone who destroys the Egyptian chariots. The call to resist tyrants is nevertheless a characteristic reading of the text—a matter not of obeying God, precisely, but of imitating Him.

III

Bondage and oppression are the key ideas in the Exodus story, but the analysis of these ideas does not exhaust the significance of Egypt. No old regime is merely oppressive; it is attractive, too, else the escape from it would be much easier than it is. The attractions of Egypt don't appear very plainly in the text, but they figure necessarily in the interpretation of the text, that is, in efforts to expand upon and explain the foreshortened, often enigmatic narrative. We can best begin, though, with a well-known passage from chapter 16 of the Book of Exodus. The Israelites have been in the wilderness now for forty-five days.

> And the whole congregation of the children of Israel mur-
> mured against Moses and Aaron. . . . And the children of

> Israel said unto them, would to God we had died by the
> hand of the Lord in the land of Egypt, when we sat by the
> fleshpots and when we did eat bread to the full.
>
> (16:2–3)

I first read this passage years ago, when I was very young, and focused then, as I shall do now, on that wonderful word "fleshpots." My attention was drawn, I confess, rather to the first part of the word than to the second; in fact, I don't remember thinking about the second at all. Nor did I ever firmly grasp, until I began working on this book, just what a fleshpot was. A prosaic object, a pot for cooking meat: even in the United States today, we sit, or most of us do, by our fleshpots. But my adolescent preoccupation with the flesh was on the mark, for meat throughout most of human history has been the food of the privileged, and "fleshpots," in the plural, doesn't refer to a lot of pots but to luxuries and sensual delights. I don't know whether the word had this meaning for the authors and editors of the Book of Exodus, or whether it came to have this meaning because of the use they made of it. In either case, we can say that the house of bondage, in the eyes of its erstwhile inhabitants, was also a land of luxury.

This became the standard view—so that generations of reformers have railed against Egyptian luxuries. Ernst Bloch takes the luxuries to be outsized and tawdry, the mirror image of modern consumer culture: "Mammoth Egypt . . . the shoddy product and symbol of the world that has come to be." In the eyes of Savonarola, Florentine "vanities" simply repeated Egyptian luxuries. Preaching on Exodus, he stressed the rich and lascivious life of the Egyptians; the promised land, the new society, would be different. The Jewish historical and interpretive literature takes a similar line. One rabbinic commentary [by Louis Ginzburg] argues, against the apparent meaning of the text, that when Pharaoh issued his command to the midwives, he was "as much interested in preserving the female children as in bringing about the death of the male children. [The Egyptians] were very sensual, and were desirous of having as many women as possible at their service." Josephus writes in the same vein in his *Antiquities of the Jews:* "The Egyptians are a nation addicted unto delicacy and impatient of labor, subject only to their pleasures." In these passages, we can hear the note of disapproval that is missing in the people's complaint about the fleshpots (though not, of course, in the narrator's report of the complaint or in Moses' reply: "Your murmurings are not against us but against the Lord"). The note of disapproval is sounded much more strongly in Leviticus and Deuteronomy and then by the Prophets. "After the doings of the land of Egypt, wherein ye dwelt, shall ye not do" (Lev. 18:3). Early Judaism is defined by its rejection not only of Egyptian bondage but also of Egyptian culture: the customary ways of the upper classes as they ate and drank, dressed and housed themselves, amused themselves, worshipped their gods, and buried their dead.

The Israelite rejection of luxury is commonly described as the response of nomads to an urban civilization. So it must have been, at least in part. A certain sort of desert puritanism survived for many centuries even after the Israelites were settled in the promised land. Thus the sect called the Rechabites, on whose doctrine Jeremiah reports:

> We will drink no wine, for Jonadab, the son of Rechab our father commanded us, saying, Ye shall drink no wine, neither ye, nor your sons forever. Neither shall ye build houses, nor sow seed, nor plant vineyards, nor have any: but all your days ye shall dwell in tents.
>
> (35:6–7)

Presumably the Rechabites ate meat—the daily manna had long since ceased—but they rejected the luxuries of urban life, and they did so from a resolutely nomadic standpoint. They were loyal to the God who spurned David's offer to build a temple: "Shalt thou build me an house for me to dwell in? Whereas I have not dwelt in any house since the time that I brought up the children of Israel out of Egypt . . . but have walked in a tent and in a tabernacle" (2 Sam. 7:5–6).

But the example of the Rechabites is not definitive for the people as a whole, who did not dream of austerity but of milk and honey. To be sure, when the Israelites celebrated their deliverance in later years, they ate matzo, "the bread of affliction," slave bread, and the eating expresses (according to a modern commentary on the Hagaddah, the prayerbook for the family observance of the Passover) "the avoidance of indulgence and arrogance . . . the simple and unspoiled life of a servant of God." But they ate the matzo, as Jews still do today, at a festive banquet, reclining on cushions, drinking wine. They "remembered" the experience of oppression while enjoying the pleasures of freedom. Nor did freedom require that they live in tents, moving with the seasons.

Desert puritanism is not a sufficient explanation for the refusal of Egyptian culture. The refusal, here and with all latter-day puritanisms, too, has to do with the complex attitude that the oppressed take toward the culture of their oppressors. The Israelites in Egypt were attracted by Egyptian life and by Egyptian worship, but in neither of these could they fully or freely share. We might think again about Exodus 16: "It does not say," as the Midrash reports, " 'when we did eat *from* the flesh pots,' but 'when we sat *by* the flesh pots.' They had to eat their bread without meat." They smelled the meat, but didn't taste it, and what they longed for in the desert was their longing in the house of bondage. But surely this kind of longing is always mixed with resentment and anger. Or, better, if some of the Israelites wanted, as the Midrash also reports, "to be like the Egyptians," others, with more pride, wanted to stress their differences and turn their backs on Egyptian "delicacies."

The commentaries are full of stories of Israelite assimilation in Egypt. "The people of Israel," said Savanarola, "became half-Egyptian." Centuries earlier, the rabbis had suggested that many Israelites dressed like Egyptians and adopted Egyptian names. They begot "strange children," reports one midrashic account, following a passage in the prophet Hosea (5:7) that is taken to mean, "they abolished the covenant of circumcision." A later Midrash, written when knowledge of Egyptian culture had long faded, interprets the line "And the land was filled with them" (Exod. 1:7) to indicate that "the amphitheaters and circuses were full of them." But the story of the bondage years is also told in an entirely different way. Some of the rabbis argued, for example, that there existed a covenant among the Israelites, years before Sinai, to preserve their ancestral customs and the memory of the God of the patriarchs. No Jew, one of them said, ever broke faith with the community of Jewish slaves in Egypt. (Who was it then who informed Pharaoh about Moses' killing of the taskmaster?) These versions of the Egyptian experience seem contradictory, but perhaps they describe different aspects of the same history. Egypt was a center of wealth and good living; it makes sense to suggest that many Israelites admired the very people who oppressed them, copied Egyptian ways, curried Egyptian favor. And other Israelites feared and repressed the impulse to act similarly in themselves.

One can trace the same tension in religious practice. The worship of idols is undoubtedly the most important of the "doings of the land of Egypt" that the Israelites were warned not to do. It is an old tradition that in Egypt they were idol worshippers, slaves imitating the religion of their masters (and not finding in it, as black slaves found in

Christianity, a gospel of freedom). Ezekiel elaborates on the flat assertion of Joshua 24 that the Israelites served strange gods "beyond the river and in Egypt."

> And they committed whoredoms in Egypt; they committed whoredoms in their youth: there were their breasts pressed, and there they bruised the teats of their virginity.
>
> (23:3)

And then the prophet threatens the people with destruction because they have brought their whoredoms with them out of Egypt into the promised land, because they have continued to go "whoring after the heathen" and because they are "polluted with their idols." The language here is the language of sexual disgust. It is most explicit in another passage from Ezekiel, describing Israel as a woman who remembers

> the days of her youth, wherein she played the harlot in the land of Egypt. For she doted upon their paramours, whose flesh is as the flesh of asses, and whose issue is as the issue of horses.
>
> (23:19–20)

This is the wrong way to remember the house of bondage, but it recalls accurately enough, perhaps, the animal gods of Egypt. Or, it refers to orgiastic forms of worship more commonly associated with the gods of Canaan. Or, it may be nothing more than a standard metaphorical reference for idol worship generally. In any case, Ezekiel can serve as a text on the sensual appeal of idolatry and the moral revulsion against it. The prophet expresses the revulsion, but recognizes the appeal: "for she doted upon their paramours." In the episode of the golden calf, . . . it is Aaron who recognizes the appeal (and perhaps succumbs to it) and Moses who expresses and then acts out the revulsion. But it is only the two together that give us Egypt through Israelite eyes.

The Israelites saw what came, later on, to be called decadence, a high culture that had gotten too high: overripe, tainted, corrupt and, at the same time, rich and alluring. In an extraordinary piece of intellectual play (in Exod. 15 and Deut. 7), the plagues with which God punished the Egyptians are turned into Egyptian diseases and made emblematic of the corruption of the land—so that going back to Egypt means, among other things, to experience the "evil diseases of Egypt."

This is the way Egypt most often figures in later revolutionary literature. A sermon by the Puritan preacher Stephen Marshall before the House of Commons in 1640 provides a typical example: "Egypt was never more bespread with locusts and frogs than our kingdom is with horrible profaneness, uncleanness, oppression, deceit, and whatsoever is a stench in the Lord's nostrils." The stench comes, I would guess, from Exodus 7, where the waters of the Nile are turned into blood: "And the river stank." What stinks in Marshall's nostrils are popish ceremonies and the rule of bishops. But we need to round out Marshall's argument with the words of another Puritan minister, who commented sadly on "the natural popery of the multitude, and of our own hearts."

One might say of the Israelites that they were natural (naturalized) Egyptians as well as rebels against Egyptian bondage and corruption. Indeed, the promised land, the opposite of bondage and corruption, is not quite as different from Egypt as I earlier suggested it was. This last point is quite deliberately conveyed in one of the more remarkable passages of the Exodus story, which describes the rebellion against Moses organized by the tribal leaders Dathan and Abiram. "Is it a small thing," these two are reported as asking, "that thou hast brought us up out of a land that floweth with milk and honey, to kill us in the wilderness?" (Num. 16:13). Egypt was, of course, a land of milk and honey, and the slaves knew that it was, even if they couldn't, or even if they wouldn't, savor its delights. And the divine promise was shaped to their consciousness—milk and honey of their own, milk and honey without the evil diseases of the Egyptians. The promised land repeats the affluence of the house of bondage, but this is supposed to be an affluence more widely shared than it was in Egypt, and it is supposed to be an affluence that doesn't corrupt. And when it isn't shared, and does corrupt, then it is time to invoke again the Exodus story.

Without the new ideas of oppression and corruption, without the sense of injustice, without moral revulsion, neither Exodus nor revolution would be possible. In the text as we have it, the new ideas are shadowed by their older opposites: the sense of injustice by resignation, revulsion by longing. The shadows are sharply drawn; this is part of the realism of the biblical story. But it is the new ideas that make the new event. They provide the energy of the Exodus, and they define its direction. The direction is definitive not only for the deliverance of Israel but for all later interpretations and applications of that deliverance. Henceforth, any move toward Egypt is a "going back" in moral time and space. When Milton wrote of the English in 1660 that they were "choosing them a captain back for Egypt," he did not mean to describe a mere return (or a cyclical repetition) but a retrogression, a "backsliding" to bondage and corruption. The slide is not incomprehensible, for Egypt is a complex reality. But it is a defeat. It is the paradigm of revolutionary defeat.

The Song of the Sea

Robert Alter

Since . . . the subject of biblical literature is not man alone but also God powerfully working in history, verse narrative could be appropriately used to represent the terrific and decisive intervention of the Lord in human affairs. In other words, there could be no proper epic poetry, with its larger-than-life human figures and its deities conceived in essentially human terms, but there could be narrative verse on a smaller scale celebrating God's power in the affairs of man, as in David's victory hymn or, preeminently, in the triumphal Song of the Sea. The Song (Exod. 15:1–18) is worth considering briefly because it provides an instance of narrative at the other end of the spectrum from the terse story of Jael. In twenty-five lines of verse, the poem moves through the whole story of the parting of the sea and the destruction of the Egyptians and onward (in a historical telescoping) through two and a half centuries involving the conquest of the Land and the establishment of the sanctuary in Jerusalem. The line divisions I offer might be contested at a couple of points: lines 13 and 14 and lines 16 and 18, which I have scanned as short lines (two beats per verset) could also be read as long lines (four beats per verset), 13 and 14 making one line and 16–18 another, triadic line, but this formal change would not substantively affect the analysis I shall propose. In any case, the division of the poem into three more or less equal strophes is clear for reasons I shall indicate in my comments, and so I have marked the ends of the strophes by a typographical break.

From *The Art of Biblical Poetry*. © 1985 by Robert Alter. Basic Books, 1985.

1	Let me sing to the Lord, Who surged, oh surged!	Horse and rider He flung into the sea.
2	My strength and power is the Lord,	and He became my saving.
3	This is my Lord, let me extol Him,	my father's God, let me exalt Him.
4	The Lord is a warrior,	the Lord is His name.
5	Pharaoh's chariots and his host	He hurled into the sea.
6	And his picked officers	were drowned in the Sea of Reeds.
7	The depths covered them,	they went down to the deep like a stone.
8	Your right hand, Lord, is mighty in power,	Your right hand, Lord, smashed the enemy.
9	In Your great surging You destroyed Your foes,	You sent forth Your wrath, You consumed them like straw.
10	In the blast of Your nostrils the waters piled high,	stood up like a wall the floods,

the depths froze in the heart of the sea.

11	The enemy said:	I'll pursue, overtake,

I'll divide the spoil

12	I'll have my fill of them,	unsheathe my sword,

my hand shall seize them.

13	You blew Your blast—	the sea covered them.
14	They sank like lead	in the mighty waters.
15	Who is like You among the gods, O Lord,	who like You, mighty in holiness,

awesome in praise, working wonders?

16	You stretched out Your hand—	the earth swallowed them.
17	You led in Your kindess	the people You redeemed.
18	You guided them in Your strength	to Your holy abode.
19	Peoples heard and quailed,	shuddering seized the dwellers of Philistia.
20	Then the chieftains of Edom panicked,	the leaders of Moab were seized with trembling.
21	All the dwellers of Canaan were dismayed,	fear and terror seized them.
22	Through the greatness of Your arm	they became like stone.
23	Until Your people passed, O Lord,	until the people passed whom You took up.
24	You brought them, planted them in the mount of Your inheritance.	A firm place for Your dwelling You made, O Lord.

A sanctuary, God, Your hands made firm.

25	The Lord shall reign	forever and ever.

The strophic division of the poem, a rare instance in biblical poetry, has long been recognized by scholarship because of the clear indications in the language of the poem. In each strophe the line before the last, or before the penultimate line, includes a nearly identical simile: "like a stone," "like lead," "like a stone." Each strophe then ends with a line celebrating God's power, and these end lines form a progression: first God's power in battle, then His might over all imagined divine beings for whom men have made claims, and finally, in a kind of *envoi*, the affirmation of His eternal sovereignty. The first strophe begins with God's "surging" (the meaning is "to triumph," but I have adopted the literal sense to retain the clear suggestion in the Hebrew of a rising tide of water), and that word begins the first line of the middle strophe as well, though it is absent at the beginning of the last strophe, perhaps because the scene of action is no longer the sea. (It might be noted, however, that a transitional continuity with the sea triumph is maintained by the stretching out of the hand at the beginning of the third strophe, the very action God had commanded Moses to perform in order to part the waters of the sea.) The first two strophes end similarly, with an image of the watery depths; the last strophe ends with an antithetical image of God's firmly or solidly founding (*konen, makhon*) a mountain abode for Himself in the Land of Israel. Within this symmetrical strophic structure, narrative momentum is developed in a particularly interesting way.

The poem begins by signaling in the first line that it is not an independent narrative but a narrative ancillary to the previously told story, and whose purpose is as much to celebrate as to narrate. Thus, the whole "plot" is already transmitted in lapidary fashion in the second verset, "Horse and rider He flung into the sea," and the subsequent telling of the tale is similarly allusive, giving first a general and elliptical account of the victory in the initial strophe, then (once more, in accord with the logic of focusing) proceeding to a more detailed rendering of the same action in the second strophe, where we get images of God's breath (that is, the wind) blowing back the water into solid columns, and dialogue that dramatizes the overweening enemy's deluded hopes of plunder and slaughter. The allied movement we have seen elsewhere in narrative verse of intensification and incremental repetition is prominent throughout this poem. One might even say that the second verset of the opening line "generates" everything in the first two strophes: the initial flinging of horse and rider becomes a drowning, a descent, a sinking of Pharaoh's chariots, his army, his choice captains, and the initial sea becomes the depths, the floods, wind-blown into walls and then back to an engulfing tide.

In this crescendo movement there is, of course, a good deal of interlinear parallelism; one particular use to which it is put—this is again a common procedure in biblical verse—is to serve as compensation for lack of semantic parallelism within the line (compare lines 5–6, 16–19). Even where there is such compensatory interlinear parallelism, one notes a tendency of the poet to forge sequential links between the parallel utterances that go on from line to line. Thus, the relation between versets in line 13, "You blew Your blast— / the sea covered them," is one of cause and effect, before and after, whereas in the next line, "They sank like lead / in the mighty waters," it is a relation between main clause and an adverbial modifier or spatial location; but the semantic parallelism between the two lines also involves temporal sequence: both depict the drowning of the Egyptians, but the wind-blown tidal wave of line 13 clearly precedes the sinking like lead in the mighty waters of the next line. Again, the pursuers' words (l. 11–12), conveyed in a nervous, two-beat triadic rhythm of urgent movement, are a clear instance of parallel acts that are also sequenced acts: pursue, overtake, divide, spoil; have my fill of them, unsheathe my sword, seize them. (In the second series, one might perhaps have expected "have my fill" at the end, but I shall not tamper with the word order of the received text in order to preserve the perfect consistency of a thesis.)

The beginning of the third strophe offers a bolder use of temporally sequenced near-synonyms because the time span involved is more than two centuries. You stretched out Your hand, You led, You guided, the poet says almost in one breath, but the three acts are, respectively, the destruction of the Egyptian host, the forty years of wandering in the wilderness, and the entry into the Land, including the ultimate fulfillment in the conquest of Jerusalem ("Your holy abode"). This telescoping effect is strikingly reinforced in the Hebrew by a phonetic assimilation of these three leading verbs involving alliteration, assonance, and rhyme—*natita, nahita, neihalta.*

The third strophe has troubled some commentators because of its patently anachronistic character: having nothing directly to do with the miraculous victory at the Reed Sea, it might even seem somehow tacked on. The theological-historical point, however, embodied in the narrative art of these verses is precisely to project out of the stunning experience at the Reed Sea a larger pattern of God's powerful—one might say "heroic"—acts in history. I would suggest that a purposeful transition is brilliantly effected at the very beginning of the last strophe with the phrase "the earth swallowed them." This obviously refers to the drowning of the Egyptians, a meaning reinforced, as I have noted, by God's repeating Moses' gesture of stretching out his hand over the sea, and also by the term 'eretz, which sometimes refers to the under-world rather than to the earth and so makes the substitution of "earth" for "sea" less problematic. But being swallowed up by the earth is reminiscent as well of the punishment of Korah's rebellious crew in one of the most memorable of the Wilderness stories and may also point forward, metaphorically rather than literally, to the fate of the Canaanites. In any case, whereas the first and second strophes begin and end with evocations of the sea, the last stanza begins by promi-nently introducing the word 'eretz—"earth," "underworld," and, most important for the end of the strophe and of the poem, "land." One might think of this transition as the application on a larger structural scale of the technique of overlap we have seen used between versets and between lines. God the destroyer of the Egyptians at the Reed Sea becomes in a single, scarcely perceptible step the guide of His people through the wilderness and into the Land, and He Who strikes with terror their enemies who would block their entrance into their prom-ised inheritance.

All this happens so fast that there is a kind of illusion of simultane-ity (or, perhaps, a kind of fiction of simultaneity), which the poet clearly exploits. It is as if the peoples of Canaan, having heard the rumors of the awesome destruction of the Egyptians, become instantly panic-stricken, long before the actual arrival of the Israelites. But the poet and his audience were perfectly aware that, by the received account, the gradual process of the conquest of the Land did not begin till forty years after the events at the Reed Sea, and the real meaning of this exercise of poetic license is to reproduce in the narrative sweep of the poem a strong and recurrent rhythm of God's action in history: just as He devastated the Egyptians, made them sink like a stone in the watery deep, His mighty presence makes the hostile nations of Canaan turn to stone with fear while He guides His people in and firmly founds His sanctuary far above the engulfing flood.

On the Divine Presence in Exodus

Leslie Brisman

For most readers of the Bible as literature, the Book of Exodus ends with chapter 34. The remaining six chapters may appear, like the ship catalogues in the *Iliad,* so much detail that we wish the inspired bard had spared us. Blake, who laid out in *Jerusalem* some visionary blue-prints analogous to those detailing the construction of the tabernacle in Exodus or the temple in Ezekiel, refused to apologize for such passages: "Every word and every letter is studied and put into its fit place," he insists in the Preface; "the terrific numbers are reserved for the terrific parts . . . and the prosaic, for inferior parts: all are necessary to each other." Whether or not we believe in such "necessity" for Ezekiel or Blake, we may be inclined to approach the "inferior parts" of Exodus as less dispensable if we regard them as part of the struggle for authority among competing traditions or authorial voices. If the Priestly, "inferior parts" reveal an effort at normalizing or institution-alizing the abiding presence of God, then the very persistence or extensity of such effort helps us appreciate the more problematic and magnificent Elohist and Yahwist passages concerning the limitedly epiphanic or anti-epiphanic nature of God.

I. THE INSTITUTIONALIZATION OF THE PRESENCE

The massive triumph of what the documentary scholars call "P," the Priestly voice, concludes with what might be specified as three

Published for the first time in this volume. © 1987 by Leslie Brisman.

distinct sublimities (as the Priestly writer understands sublimities)—three variations on the idea of God's abiding presence. First, there is the stately passage as the orders for the construction of the Temple are carried out in seven units, each punctuated by the formula, "as the Lord had directed Moses" (40:16–33). This, together with the phrase *vayichal Moshe* ("Moses finished the work"), suggests the seven days of the Priestly writer's story of Creation, each punctuated with *vayichal Elohim* ("God finished the work"). It is possible to label this a sublimity of style, since it involves the transvaluation of rather dull Tabernacle business, the fulfillment of previously specified directions, into something as decorous and momentous as the Creation. Informing the sublimity of style is a sublimity of Priestly thought—the thought that the "work" of the tabernacle is an image of the "work" of Creation. Both nature and worship are given mythological origins, representations of when they first occurred; both are understood to be ongoing. Beyond similitude there is, thus, an implied pious synecdoche: man's worship represents an ongoing opportunity to participate in the work of Creation; for this Priestly writer, addressing a people to be "a kingdom of priests," religious institution shares in cosmic invention.

Skipping the second sublimity for a moment, we can point to the last three verses of Exodus as a Priestly adaptation of the Yahwist vision of history—of a God who once accompanied the Israelites on their way and who may still be imagined to "dwell among them" in a centralized house of worship. The cloud of Yahweh that rests on the Tabernacle by day in the last verse of Exodus is not quite the pillar of cloud that the Yahwist imagined going before the people during the day (Exod. 13:22). Because the Priestly vision maps God at the center of the camp, we may be led to regard the Priestly cloud and fire as an introversion of the Yahwist's two pillars that were to go before and stand outside the camp. In the adaptation of the older tradition to Priestly concerns, we can read a statement of faith in the continuity of Divine Presence. That Presence is seen to transcend particular source strata and particular historical event or religious institution. The God who accompanied the people before the Tabernacle and then by means of the Tabernacle will continue with them (Exodus implies as the book breaks off) when Tabernacle becomes Temple. Ezekiel (11:16) will extend the vision of mobile Divine Presence to include post-Temple days and the origins of what we more properly conceive as Judaism.

Exodus thus concludes with a version of the thought that God is with the community in its ongoing, historical existence and not just in isolated moments of revelation to the present community's ancient heroes. Such is also the thought that concludes the Gospel of Matthew, for example, when Jesus makes a brief reappearance to proclaim, "Know that I am with you always; yea, till the end of time" (28:20). I turn to the New Testament for a reminder of how profound is the need for, and the privileging of, this mode of transcendence. All the incarnations in the world will not fill the human appetite for the Paraclete—for a sense of the Divine as present now when ostensibly absent. In the Pentateuch, the promise "I shall be with you" is made by God to Jacob (Gen. 26:3; 31:3) and reiterated to Moses (Exod. 3:4) and Joshua (Deut. 31:23). It is notable that all three of these Pentateuchal promises of the ongoing Presence of God are J texts, as is the Exodus text that first figures that Presence to the collective Israelites in the form of a pillar of cloud by day and a pillar of fire by night (13:21–22). When the pillar of cloud and pillar of fire return at the end of Exodus, they are now more truly representative of the abiding Presence, for they abide over the tabernacle in a way that suggests the sanction of post-Mosaic religious institution rather than the mere description of an event in the desert. The Priestly fire and cloud seem less literal, more "metaphysical," more like symbols of God dwelling "in the midst" of the people (Lev. 26:11–12). Thus the sublimity of the final representation of the abiding Presence of God in Exodus is related to the knowledge we have of the co-option of some J iconography, very beautiful in its original context but functioning there to do something other, perhaps something less. If we regard the compositional strands of the Pentateuch not simply as a succession of texts but a competition of voices, we can say of the recurrence of that fire and cloud that it represents the overwhelming victory of the Priestly voice. The pillar of fire and cloud are spoils of the conquest. They are taken over from J by P and made to stand, at the very end of Exodus, for the triumph of Priestly vision. This sense of appropriation might be made clearer by considering the possibility that Isa. 6:3 includes a piece of what was already temple doxology or that Rev. 4:8 includes the already liturgical *Sanctus*. If an old piece of J narrative about pre-Tabernacle wanderings can become part of the Priestly vision of Tabernacle business, then all narrative, including narratives about revelation, can be fit into the liturgical perspective of a later era. I should like to show as well that old philosophical differences can be fit into new narrative contexts so that differences in outlook emerge as episodes in a historical stream.

Just before the last three verses of Exodus and their representation of ongoing, priestly activity, we have two remarkable verses that constitute what we may single out as an independent sublimity. In contrast to the last three verses of Exodus, these two verses seem to refer to a unique happening: "The cloud covered the tent of meeting and the glory of the Lord filled the tabernacle. Moses could not enter the tent of meeting because the cloud abode thereon and the glory of the Lord filled the tabernacle." Here the sense of God as *beyond* human activity is troped as the presence of God *before* human activity: Filling that tabernacle, God prevents ("goes before" and thwarts) Moses from filling his duty. It is a happy prevention, this dedicatory vision of the presence of God. Earlier, the Priestly account of the furnishing of the Tabernacle included the construction of two cherubim on the covering of the ark, cherubim whose outspread wings would define a space, one might say "hold a space" for the absent, nonspatial deity. But at the end of Exodus, God's presence fills not just the well-defined limits of the "mercy seat" above the ark but the whole Tabernacle. To appreciate how remarkable a vision this is, and especially how remarkable a Priestly vision, we need only to consider the denunciation of priestly activity in Ezekiel 28. Allegorically represented by the king of Tyre, the high priest is called a *kruv mimshach,* an extended (overextended) cherub who, in corrupt pride, fills the Temple with the self-arrogating role of the priest; he fills the Temple with himself. For the Priestly writer to conclude Exodus with a vision of God filling the Tabernacle, he needs to look beyond the priestly business of God's work to a vision of the Divine Presence that prevents and overwhelms the priesthood—and even Moses himself.

I want to conclude the brief look at the Priestly sublimities on that note in order to contrast the vision of the divine as *mimshach,* widespreading Presence, with the more characteristic human *nimshach,* or "drawn in" concern. In the end, the Priestly writer gives us one glimpse of a deity whose power to "take up space" means the power to overwhelm, to exclude, to keep Moses and Aaron waiting. But until the end of Exodus, what we get instead might be called a conflict of human powers, each rushing in to take up space—special, sacred space—so that our sense of the presence of a particular documentary strand may overwhelm our sense of Divine Presence. My subject is the clash of voices over the question of the presence of God. From a perspective that we might label "neo-pietistic," the discovery of the documentary nature of the Pentateuch is no more alarming than the discovery that the four Gospels are written by men with different religious outlooks; from the neo-pietistic perspective, the documentary nature of Exodus is like the existence of cherubim whose gold substance is one with the mercy seat between them: The voice of Yahweh is heard "between" them, just as the figure of Jesus emerges "between" or among the Gospels. From a different perspective, the J, E, and P voices of Exodus are not so much guardian cherubs as covering cherubs, each seeking to spread its wing over and define the space of God's presence as (what for simplicity's sake we can specify as) J space, E space, or P space. It is almost certain that the documentary history of Exodus is more complicated than that of the Synoptic Gospels—that we have not just three writers but a host of redactional hands each, like senators adding riders to a bill, inserting his own notion of revelation, Divine Presence, or the meaning of a particular tradition; but it is often convenient to personify schools of thought as the individuals—as though the dominance of P at the end of Exodus, for example, represented a priestly individual having the last word in a quarrel with E and J.

Before attempting to show exegesis become preemption within Exodus itself, I turn to two exemplary representations of exegetical preemption of space at the borders of our text but outside it. I want to pick one Christian and one Jewish "covering cherub" not to make the point that both Christians and Jews cover or obscure the text (as though one could isolate some original, core text free of such coverings) but to represent how alluring is the temptation, and how imaginative the results of such preemption. The Christian might be represented by a magnificent painting of Nicholas Froment showing the scene of the burning bush in Exod. 3:2. Froment puts Moses and his sheep in the earthly foreground, while the center of the picture, beyond "our world," opens the burning bush to reveal the Virgin Mary with the baby Jesus. If the Bible is indeed one book, the inappropriateness of having *that* God revealed to Moses is more than compensated for by the (literally) preposterous revelation of the Redeemer to come. God's revelation, "I know their sorrows; and I am come down to deliver them out of the hand of the Egyptians" (3:7–8) seems but a figure for the grand assumption of sorrows and once-for-all deliverance when the Messiah is sent instead of Moses and the cross replaces the bush.

On the other side, consider the talmudic exegesis of Exod. 33:23. What did Moses see when God passed before him and Moses saw his "back"? He saw the prayer-leader, with his *tallit* drawn over his head in pious concentration, intoning the passage that Jewish liturgy quotes from Exodus 34: "The Lord, the Lord, gracious and compassionate God, slow to anger, abounding in mercy and truth; keeping mercy for thousands, forgiving iniquity, transgression, and sin, and wiping the slate clean." This is not the only talmudic passage where God Himself is imagined in prayer, calling upon His own merciful nature. But it is especially remarkable to find the liturgical adaptation—i.e., a later historical development, cited (however playfully) as the biblical passage's "source."

While neither of these interpretations could be said to remain within the bounds of what we ordinarily regard as literary interpretation (as opposed to homiletic or midrashic invention), both respond with remarkable clarity to a craving for Divine Presence that the text itself, in contrast, complicates or puts far off. When Moses first asks God to name Himself, God resists the request to make his name (and his nature) "present" to Moses; what he says is *eheyeh asher eheyeh*, "I will be what I will be!"—that is all ye know on earth and all ye need to know. The Christian vision of a New Testament inherent in the old may be represented by that babe in the bush, as though the Christian reader, knowing the whole story, could finish God's sentence for him: "I will be—the incarnate Christ!" The Jewish vision of talmudic wisdom "given to Moses at Sinai" may be represented by that capsule vision of what Moses requested to see when he besought God, "Show me your glory!" God reveals to Moses an image of rabbinic Judaism. Both these images, the baby Jesus and the cantor repeating the attributes of divine compassion, are images of the "mercy seat" occupied. They are images, that is, not only of Divine Presence but of the ultimate benignity of Divine Presence as manifest in the later history of the cult.

I think it is fair to say that the writers of Exodus longed equally for the revelation of Divine Presence as an ultimate benignity; but whether their wished-for future corresponded to their notion of the Sinaitic past is more complex. In what follows I want to look more closely at some of the complexities attending each of these passages, the preliminary revelation of Divine Presence to Moses in Exodus 3, and the revisionary aura of the very tangled revelations in chapters 33–34. We should note first, however, that the two passages themselves stand as something of a pair of cherubim on either side of the revelation or revelations on Sinai associated with the public theophany and the first set of tablets of the law.

II. THE FIRST THEOPHANY

Like Moses, the reader of Exodus receives a series of first lessons in revelation at Horeb in chapter 3. One of these lessons is the surprisingly dialogic nature of revelation. Here Moses argues with God about unworthiness and (it seems) impels a revelation not otherwise forthcoming. In chapter 19 Moses again speaks boldly, this time reminding God of God's own prohibitions and previous directives (19:23). Perhaps the single most beautiful verse in the entire description of a first encounter at Sinai suggests that at the limit of human capacity to imagine revelation is that mode of speech we ordinarily contrast with it—conversation: "A trumpet-like voice grew louder and louder; Moses spoke, and God voiced a response" (19:19). Some translate *bikol* as "with thunder," but this surely misses the point that God's presence is manifest in His voice, His beneficence in His willingness to assume the respondent's role, the *answering* voice. Following the episode of the golden calf and throughout the negotiations over a second revelation, Moses' willingness to speak up—to converse with, and even argue with God—becomes of paramount importance. Moses not only is permitted to appear to generate God's recantation, but he provokes (in the root sense of "calling forth"—or perhaps in the literal sense of himself calling out) the statement of divine mercy and forbearance in chapter 34.

If the first lesson is "Thou shalt talk back!," the second is "Thou shalt interrupt!" Until we get to the silencing of all opposition in the Priestly chapters that conclude Exodus, interruption is more the order of the day than the exception. Indeed, even the passage in chapter 20 which we have come to regard as the Decalogue seems to be an interruption in a story that was headed somewhere else. And that is only one of several passages of law and narrative that interrupt each other and compete for attention on the scene of revelation. In the Call Scene (as we might term chap. 3) Moses' question, "When they say to me, 'What is His name?' what shall I tell them?" seems to have once had a straightforward answer: God said to Moses, "Say this to the Children of Israel: 'Yahweh, the God of your fathers, the God of Abraham, the God of Isaac, and the God of Jacob sent me to you.' That is my name forever and that is how I am to be remembered" (3:15).

If a midrashic hand "opened" the text between such a question and such an answer, inspiration and *chutzpah* are near allied. What more inviting, more daring place to add something new than when all ears are poised to hear God's voice? Our narrative ostensibly poses the question "Who are you?"—or "What are you?" since the name and nature of God are near allied. We expect, that is, the following verse to be an expression of the presence of God; what we find, in verse 14, appears to be the presence of another writer—and a verse that proclaims not the presence but the deferred presence of God. If we understand the phrase *eheyeh asher eheyeh* to mean literally what it says, not "I am that I am" but "I will be what I will be," then Moses' request for a definitive name is a request rebuffed before it is (in the old verse announcing "Yahweh, the God of your fathers") answered in the conventional manner.

Beyond sheer exuberance—exuberance that is itself a revelation of power—the new answer defies the request for name by making the denial of name, the denial of present manifestation, a truer revelation of the nature of the deity. God is the One Who Is Deferred, the One who will be whatever He pleases, the One Who will be with whomever He pleases. Perhaps we capture the sense of nonanswer that God tells Moses to give the Israelites if we paraphrase *eheyeh shilachani aleichem* (literally, "*I Will Be* has sent me before you") as "I Will Be Whoever I Damn Please."

There is a rabbinic midrash which explains that Moses' failure to appreciate the promise in verse 12, "I will be with you," is responsible for the hardly benevolent theophany in 4:24. Such filling in of a most startling narrative gap is based on an analogy between Moses returning from Jethro and Jacob returning from Laban. Both heroes express a doubt about the guaranteed "I will be with you"—Jacob by taking such strategic precautions before meeting Esau, Moses by requesting a further revelation of God's name. Both are symbolically reproved for their lack of trust in the One Not Present by being made to confront an all-too-present form of God's wrath, an angel whose aggression against the hero, once overcome or appeased, confirms the hero in his progress along the appointed route. One might suppose that the function of such midrashim is to serve as a kind of Jacobic disguise: one puts them on in order to experience the illusion, when they are removed, of a smooth text (however Jacobic and tricky) free of excremental (wild, Esau-like) addition. But what the midrash exposes instead is the illusion that there is a smooth text one layer beneath midrashic addition. Indeed, so great is the bond between the promise "I will be with you" in 4:12 and the play on Yahweh's name in verse

14 that these together seem to separate themselves from the "straightforward" answer of verse 15. We begin to wonder if verse 15, beginning with the words "God also said to Moses," does not constitute the
addition, the excrementitious hair on which too weak a faith has been
hung. That is, although several scholars of the documentary hypothesis tell us that the "also" of "God also said to Moses" indicates that an
insertion has been made and that what follows the "also" is original,
the effect of reading the text as we have it, especially the effect after
considering and discarding further midrashic layers, is to regard the
also as precisely that, the introduction of secondary material.

Is it possible truly to know the historical cause for this literary
effect? Is it possible, that is, to tell whether a writer we call E has been
interrupted by a later midrashist or whether E (or J!) is the creator of
the magnificent verse 14, after which follows an old line or a pious
redactor's attempt at filling in the old line, the expected and more
normative response by God to Moses? From a literary standpoint,
what is *original* in the sense of "inspired" is the midrashic play with the
divine name in verse 14. There can be no recovery of a pre-midrashic
text because the story without verse 14 omits a powerful (*and in that
sense genuine*) revelation of Yahweh's distaste for being nameable, de-
finable, predictable.

Regardless of what view one ultimately takes of the discontinuity
of the text at this juncture, the question of primary and secondary
compositional strata is related in a curious way to the questions about
the primary or secondary nature of God's presence. Does the angel of
Yahweh who appears to Moses in verse 2 belong to the same text as
the voice of God that calls Moses in verse 4? Some scholars complicate
the difference further by assuming that a pious scribe has substituted
"angel of Yahweh" where the J author boldly wrote "Yahweh." But
with or without *angel,* the text as we have it contains at least two
different views of God's presence in that bush—and two different
views of God's continued presence to Moses. We can call *Yahwist* the
idea that Yahweh is somehow present in that bush and will be directly
taking part in the history to come: "I have come down to deliver [my
people] from the hand of Egypt and to bring it up from that land to
the great good place." (3:8). From an Elohist perspective, the real
question about God's unmediated presence does not concern angel or
no angel; God is never manifest except as a voice, and Moses' pious
gesture in hiding his face in verse 6 does not imply that God Himself
could be physically perceived by someone who did not avert his

glance. Similarly, the difficult questions posed in chapters 23 and 33 about an angel of Yahweh vs. Yahweh Himself as the guiding spirit are not Elohist questions. But there is a real, Elohist question about the role of Moses as savior. From a documentary perspective, verses 7–9a may be a J text and verses 9b–13 an E text, each with its own account of the same narrative fact—the promise of redemption. But from what we might label a "midrashic" perspective, the E account appears to be not an alternative to but a refinement on the Yahwist passage. It is as though the Elohist passage returns to the question of Moses' role in God's plan of redemption, and by traversing that ground more slowly, rolls back a veil and uncovers a new spiritual reality. More precisely, the Elohist passage has God say to Moses, "Come now, I will send you to Pharaoh and you will bring my people, the Children of Israel, from Egypt" (4:10). Moses himself then seems to linger over the words, as though asking, "What do you mean *I* will bring your people forth from Egypt?" This question prompts the crucial statement of God's presence: "I will be with you." In this way, even the Elohist strand itself is inherently midrashic, and seems to conjure into manifestation the Divine Presence it describes by opening a space in a hypothetical ur-text.

What follows the promise of God's presence is so strange that many have supposed the text corrupt. At least one translation even prints ellipses dots to indicate the omission of an expected specification: " 'I shall be with you' was the answer, 'and this is the sign by which you shall know that it is I who have sent you. . . . After you have led the people out of Egypt, you are to offer worship to God on this mountain.' " So unusual is it to have the word *ot* mean "sign" in the sense of directional sign, a pointer towards a proper course rather than "wonder" or "supernatural proof," that the E text is imagined to have once offered a wonder that assures Moses of God's presence and promise, *after which* God goes on to specify that upon Moses' leading the people forth from Egypt, they will worship God on this very mountain. One medieval exegete proposes that after the words "and this is the sign" God shows Moses the pillar of cloud, and this sign, together with the fire of the burning bush, points forward to the Divine Presence accompanying the people in the desert. The more usual hypothesis is that the *zeh* (the "this") refers to the burning bush. Perhaps the most brilliant such reading is the form-critical analysis of Brevard Childs, according to which the words "and this is the sign" were once followed by the revelation of the burning bush. When this

text was then redacted with a Yahwist account which had the introduction of the burning bush *precede* the Call Narrative, the pointer,
"this is the sign" was left dangling; the pronoun refers to what is,
unforgettably, already there.

Whether or not Childs's argument about the prehistory of the text
can be believed, it is clear that in the text as we have it, chapter 3 elides
the sort of sign-as-magic-show that the old J text of chapter 4 provides. There Yahweh even specifies the force of the signs as their
"voice" (4:8), a figure that intensifies the contrast to the pure voice of
Divine Presence in the Elohist passage in 3:12. And as we have it,
3:12 does not seem to point back to the burning bush but forward to
the theophany yet to come after the Exodus. It is as though an Elohist
redactor rewrote the theophany to emphasize the same spiritual message that is encoded in verse 14's substituting "I will be" for "Yahweh."
In verse 11, Moses asks "Who am I?" and is answered with two turns
away from the present to the future: I *will be* with you; and as for
signs, the only sign you need is the directive, the sign that points
forward: after you have brought the people out of Egypt, you are to
worship God on this mountain. What we have, then, in the verses that
lead up to the awesome evasion of God's name, is a conversation with
Moses already filled with deferment and evasion of unmediated presence. The proclamation, "I will be what I will be" may, in terms of
the composition of the text, interrupt what was once whole; but in
terms of the reading of the text, this revelation brings to a fitting
climax an Elohist theme of deferment. Even *the* moment of God's
presence at Sinai will be figured by the Elohist as a conversation
perfectly imaging God's presence to Moses because it mysteriously
captures the quality of time put off: *Moshe yidaber vahaelohim yaanehu
bikol*—"Moses would speak and God would answer him," a grammatical imperfect identical to a grammatical—and prophetic—perfect future: "Moses will speak and God will answer him" (19:19).

III. REVELATION REVISITED

It is a shocking thing, as Yehezkel Kaufmann has argued, that the
Old Testament so repeatedly misrepresents the nature of idolatry: idols
were generally not mistaken for the gods themselves, and it would be
more accurate to represent the difference between Israel and her neighbors as the difference over the question of whether it is permissible to
employ icons to represent a divinity. In the golden calf episode, the

people seem to cry out for visible manifestations of God rather than for a different god, and Moses, the other mediator they know besides the pillar of fire and pillar of cloud, is also absent: "We do not know what has become of him" (32:1).

Chapter 32 concludes with a blaze of Yahwist anger—a bitterly ironic reminder of what too eager an insistence on Yahweh's tangible presence might mean. Chapter 33 introduces a series of meditations on the loss of Divine Presence, a series all the more poignant for involving (like *Lycidas,* for example) what at first appears to be less consistency as a narrative sequence than growing intensity of focus on the implications of the loss.

The first such passage, or the first cluster of such passages, concerns the people's collective transformation of mistake into mourning. We are not told that the Children of Israel repented of the golden calf—perhaps because the random decimation of three thousand calf-worshipers comes so speedily that it preempts a change of heart. Nor do we linger over the question of whether the people were indeed worshiping another god or mistaking their absent deity for one or ones declared by Aaron to be present in the calf/calves. (The confusion about singular or plural is wondrous in itself, regardless of whether its source is the transformation of Jeroboam's two golden calves [1 Kings 12:28] into a myth of their origin.) Instead of lingering over the question of the absence of God or the absence of faith in a God not visibly present, the text substitutes a second trauma that "screens" the first: anxiety about God's "absence" as the people wait at Sinai becomes the grief over God's absence from the midst of the people from this time forth. This turn, from a faithless anxiety to a legitimate grief, might be said to inspire the turn to a notion of God's continued absence. Just a few verses before (32:34, recapitulating a theme of 23:23, though one or even both passages may be editorial additions) the angel of Yahweh guiding the people seemed to be a trope for God's presence. Now (33:2-3) the angel is a trope of absence: A second-order guide replaces the unimaginable "original." I think we can speak of the revision of Sinaitic absence into desert absence as fairly certain. Less certain is a second revision, the stripping of ornaments. Whatever the textual history of the passage may be, it appears to the reader of the text we have that "originally" the stripping of ornaments enjoined by a wrathful of Yahweh; the people's decision to remove their ornaments as a sign of mourning looks like an inspired revision. But the major revision is that of focus: The loss of God's unmediated presence in the desert march to come is a loss they can feel in a way they could not feel the loss (or the responsibility for the loss) of Divine Presence during the giving of the law at Sinai.

If the first "meditation on the loss of Divine Presence" may also be called the people's, then the second might be labeled the priest's. I do not mean that 33:7–11 is a Priestly text. It is clearly not that (since the passage contradicts everything the Priestly text tells us about the Tabernacle, including the fact that it is yet to be built). But this passage does return us to a vision of ongoing worship, a vision of Divine Presence as it is imagined to be accommodated to history, to the "real world" of religious institution. Whatever the original context of the passage may have been, the effect of inserting it here is to draw the most radical antithesis between the blazing anger of the too-much-present Yahwist God and the ever-transcendent deity who is outside the camp and approachable only through the mediation of Moses. But it is not just two visions of God that are thrown into contrast; the passage likewise contrasts with the narrative problem that surrounds it (the problem about what do with the question of God's presence) a moment of pure vision into an untroubled world. Beyond narrative— beyond, that is, a history of troubles in the relation of God to man— stands this dream of ongoing, efficacious Mosaic mediation and a people at ease with an approachable God. Although the passage is probably drawn from the Elohist source that gave us Moses conversing with God on Sinai (19:19), the effect of placing the passage here is to suggest not a continuation but an alternative to Sinai as well as the golden calf. In a world where "Yahweh would speak to Moses face to face, as a man speaks to his friend," there is no need for Sinai; in a world where all the people, observing the meeting of Moses and God, "stand each one in the door of his tent and bow," there is no possibility of a cry for a calf. More particularly, in a world where Moses goes out to the Tent of Meeting *and returns* (verse 11) in full sight of all the people, there is no room for the apprehension about the Divine Presence or the mediator's whereabouts—apprehension that, outside this golden vision, led to apostasy. If chapter 33 could be said to collect elegiac responses to a sense of loss, verses 7–11 constitute the flower passage, what Milton called the "false surmise" or dalliance with a beautiful dream of what is not to be.

The passage that follows (vv. 12–17) returns to the world of the Fall. We are brought back not only to the narrative place in time (after the calf) but to the Yahwistic narrative situation of a Moses bargaining with God. Perhaps we should even say "wrestling" rather than "bargaining," for there is something in the verbal tension that suggests not just Abraham politely cheapening the price of the redemption of Sodom but Jacob struggling with that angel in the dust. When Yahweh says in verse 5, "Now take off your ornaments and I'll know what to do with you," he sounds like a wrestler saying "take your glasses off." Moses' bargaining chip comes from Yahwist play on the divine terms. *Hored edyicha* (literally "lower your ornaments") suggests the contrast between this "lowering" and the assured "raising" of the people to the land of Canaan (vv. 1, 12). The Yahwist's Moses couples this verbal audacity with a scrutiny of Yahweh's verbs of knowledge. What do you mean, "I'll know what to do with you?" and what *did* you mean by "I know you by name"? You have not made known to me whom you will send with me, and you have not made known to me your ways. You have said "You have found favor in my eyes," but now let *me* get to know *you* so that I might better find favor in your eyes.

Moses' audacity is matched by a remarkably oracular divine pronouncement: *Panai yelechu vahanichoti lach,* which we generally translate along the lines of "My Presence shall accompany you and I will give you rest." But Moses is cautious about interpreting this promise, and we need to take a hint from him. We need to keep in mind that the Hebrew for "Presence" is literally "face," so that the revelation promised Moses at the conclusion of the chapter—that he would see God's "back"—clearly points to something else. In English we can speak of "the presence of God in history," though the more usual idiom may be "the hand of God." In Hebrew, at least in the Yahwist's Hebrew, the theophanic Presence needs to be distinguished from a more abstract presence discernable only in overview, from the perspective of the end (Hebrew "back") of days. The second word, *yelechu,* is no less tricky. English translations render it "accompany" or "go with," though the Hebrew only means "go." One possible meaning of Yahweh's pronouncement is "My Presence will go [go away]; I will leave you alone." We think we know that *yelechu* means "go along with, go in front of"; but we, or at least Moses, wants to be sure. Similarly *hanichoti* usually means giving rest in the sense of setting Moses' mind at rest, seeing him to the end of the journey; but we have seen enough of Yahweh's threatened abandonment of His backsliding people to raise the possibility that the rest promised Moses is a loss: If you do not stop bothering me, I'll go away. And finally, the *lach* suggests a source of legitimate anxiety given what we have seen before. It presumably refers to Moses as a synecdoche for the house of Israel: I will give you all your rest in bringing you to the land of Canaan. But this singular "you" may also raise the specter of Moses' personal redemption without that of the people at large.

Against all these ambiguities, Moses' assertive "bargaining" clears a path. First comes the ultimatum: "If your Presence doesn't go, we don't go; don't bother budging us from this spot." I see no reason to suppose that this strongly voiced condition has been misplaced, that it once preceded God's assurance He would accompany them and grant rest. On the contrary, the placement of Moses' most audacious appeal to God reflects the nagging of the issue of what "presence" means. Insisting on God's presence, Moses gets to restate the idiom so as to insure that "going" means "going along with us" and that the "us" includes not just Moses or Moses and the Levites but the Children of Israel collectively. The pericope ends with Yahweh's accession to Moses' demands and vocabulary: "I will do all you say because [as you say] you have found favor in my eyes and I have known you by name."

What is the relation between being on a first-name basis and knowing the nature of one's intimate acquaintance? It is possible that at this point we are to recall Yahweh's dodging of Moses' question about name in chapter 3, for the evasion "I will be what I will be" looks very much like the promise of a glimpse of Yahweh's back. Indeed, the connotation in chapter 3, "I will not be bound by you!" becomes more explicit in chapter 33: "I will be gracious to whom I will be gracious, and will show mercy on whom I will show mercy" (33:19). If we understand *name* to be a figure of speech for *nature,* Moses' new audacity ("Show me your glory") and his old ("Tell me your name!") are the same. Not a private foible, a reach beyond public role into request for private vision, the attempt to understand the nature of God slides into the attempt to privilege the merciful and salvific side of God's nature. Whether or not this is what Moses means when he requests, "Show me your glory!" this is how Yahweh chooses to answer him: "I will pass all My goodness before you." The terms of the conversation have shifted from *presence* to *glory* to *goodness.* Even if the three terms could be shown to be relics of three textual strands (and I do not think they are), what we have in the redacted text is a symbolic progress from theophany to theology.

If we follow this "progress" beyond the bounds of the Book of Exodus, we find, in Christianity, an incarnate God giving way to a

Paraclete or more generally a Christ giving way to a Kingdom of God diffused "among you." In Judaism the absence of a single figure of messianic presence leads either to Isaiah's innovation, the Israelites *as* a messianic figure, or to the uncannily human God who is imaged to be "with" His people in suffering with them. The transmutation of the idea of Divine Presence among the prophets and in postbiblical times is a separate set of subjects whose complexity I betray in attempting to touch on it here, but a passage from Isaiah may illuminate the sort of midrashic revisionary activity that I am claiming we can find in Exodus itself. The Masoretic text of Isa. 62:11 proclaims the coming of salvation (*savior* in the Greek) while the savior of the past is remembered as being no less than God Himself. According to the Masoretic text (with a little help from an editorial substitution of *lo* ("to him" for its homonym meaning "not"), God was with the people in all their troubles; the presence of an angel saved them. The Septuagint allows us to glimpse what is undoubtedly an earlier version of the text: "In all their troubles, not a mediator or angel; His Presence saved them—in His love and mercy He saved them." Perhaps the rabbis, not having the Greek, interpreted and punctuated as they did because the word *tzar*, so close to *tzarotam,* suggested that "their trouble" was His "trouble." But the easier emendation is that which yields an original text that takes us back to Exodus 33. God's mercy is shown by His willingness to accede to Moses' request, to forget about substituting a minister or angel and to allow *panav,* His face, His Presence, to accompany the people and save them.

The rabbinic vision of a human, all-too-human God who suffers with His people may be a revision that turns human suffering into pathos and apparent disappearance of God into the poignant thought of distant identification. But Exodus itself, while insisting on the continued presence of God, already revises the "face" into an "aspect," the Presence into a theological *view.* With the completion or renewal of the giving of the law in Exodus 34 comes the crucial retroping of the Presence of God as His *presence in the law.* Whether or not Harold Bloom is right about the Yahwist's Yahweh being so Coriolanus-like in His distaste for public exposure in chapter 19 [see the essay in this volume], the injunction repeated in chapter 34 that no one is to accompany Moses or be seen anywhere on the mountain is an injunction that takes us somewhere else. It takes us beyond Yahweh's "personality" (the distaste of a person for exposing his person) into the attributes of God. What is revealed in revelation is not the visual form of deity nor the "body" of law; it is the set of divine attributes by which He is to be invoked or conceived—really just one attribute, but phrased as *asseret hadibrot,* the Ten Names:

> Yahweh, Yahweh is (1) a merciful God and (2) compassion-
> ate, (3) slow to anger, (4) full of lovingkindness and (5)
> truth, (6) keeping in mind lovingkindness for thousands, (7)
> forgiving iniquity and (8) transgression and (9) sin; (10) He
> will not utterly destroy.

The last phrase is always translated along the lines of "He will not utterly forgive," or "He will by no means clear the guilty," on the assumption that it introduces the following qualification to God's mercy: "He visits the iniquity of the fathers upon the children and the children's children, to the third and the fourth generation." But I wonder if such a qualification is not a later insertion on the part of a theologian who could make no sense of God's presence and God's mercy. Solution? "God is always 'present' in the sense that He registers and takes action; but He chooses not to strike back with perfect aim and sometimes hits as far away as the third or fourth generation." I paraphrase as vulgarly as I can because I believe the thought vulgar and no part of the Ten Attributes. The rabbis knew as much when they made the Ten Attributes the basis of prayer, but cut them off with the word *nakeh,* thus retaining the "clearing" of the guilty before the rest of the phrase which makes it subject to the translation "He will by no means clear the guilty." I believe Jeremiah too understood the attri-butes as I do when he explained messianism as the salvific presence of God: *Ki itcha ani*—"I am with you" and will not utterly destroy you (*vinakeh lo anakecha*). It is, of course, possible to say that Jeremiah (or the deutero-Jeremiah we conventionally assimilate to the prophet by that name) is in 30:11 quoting Exodus 34 to revise the meaning of the phrase and turn the sternness of "I will by no means forgive the guilty" into the benevolence of "I will by no means wipe you out." But I believe, rather, that he is quoting Exodus 34 as he understood it. The presence of God might have meant, given the irascible nature of the Yahwist's Yahweh, just the show of angry force that Moses works so hard to avert. The prophet restores a vision of a god whose presence is his benevolence.

I have argued that the idea of God holding a grudge to the third or fourth generation is an editorial addition—an attempt to solve the reward and punishment dilemma perhaps especially peculiar when seen not just from this side of the golden calf episode but from this side of the Christian solution, the proposal of a world elsewhere in which the calculations come out right. I am aware of how far the Grudge Idea (usually called "vicarious punishment") has metastasized throughout the Old Testament and how shaky the evidence for its being something other than a zaniness of the Yahwist. My suggestion does not find a place in Michael Fishbane's monumental study of interpolated commentary, *Biblical Interpretation in Ancient Israel;* he defends the antiquity and unity of the formula in 34:6–7 as opposed to transformations of it elsewhere. Yet whether or not the Grudge Idea is an example of the *nimshach,* of ideas drawn onto the scene of revelation by later hands, it is clear that the list of divine attributes emphasizes not the limits but the extent of God's mercy. Whatever the documentary history of the passage as we have it, the passage comes, in the narrative history, as a revelation of the god-to-be. Yahweh was a god who did not like to be seen, "understood," or told what to do. To see His "face" is to look *lifanim*—literally "to the face," idiomatically "to look at the history of what is 'before' us"; and what is "before us" is the golden calf and the strong retribution it provokes. To see His "back" is to look ahead to the divine attributes. Yahweh *was* a consuming fire; henceforth the presence of the Lord will be evoked in the faith that, although He will be what He will be, He will be something else.

Chronology

HISTORICAL

The Creation and the Flood

?	The Creation and the Flood
1800 B.C.E.	The Patriarchs and the Sojourn in Egypt (ca. 1800–1250)
1700 B.C.E.	
1600 B.C.E.	
1500 B.C.E.	
1400 B.C.E.	
1300 B.C.E.	
1200 B.C.E.	The Exodus and the Conquest (ca. 1250–1200)
	Joshua (ca. 1200–1150)
	The Judges (ca. 1150–1025)
1100 B.C.E.	
1000 B.C.E.	The Monarchy (ca. 1025–930)
	The Two Kingdoms (ca. 930–590)

The J Source (ca. 950–900)

123

TEXTUAL		HISTORICAL
The E Source (ca. 850–800)	900 B.C.E.	
	800 B.C.E.	
Amos, Proverbs 10–22:16 (ca. 750)		
Hosea (ca. 725)		The Fall of Samaria (ca. 720)
Micah, Proverbs 25–29, Isaiah 1–31, JE redaction (ca. 700)	700 B.C.E.	The Reformation of Josiah (ca. 700–600)
Deuteronomy, Zephaniah (ca. 650)		
Nahum, Prov. 22: 17–24 (ca. 625)		
Deuteronomy–Kings (ca. 600–500), Jeremiah, Habakkuk (ca. 600)	600 B.C.E.	The Fall of Jerusalem and the Exile to Babylonia (ca. 587–538)
Job 3–31, 38–42:6 (ca. 575)		
Isaiah 40–55, Job 32–37 (ca. 550)		The Return (ca. 538)
Isaiah 56–66, Jeremiah 46–52, Ezekiel 1–37, 40–48, Lamentations (ca. 525)		
Job redaction, the P Source, Haggai, Zechariah 1–8, Jeremiah 30–31 (ca. 500)	500 B.C.E.	
Additions to Ezekiel 1–37, 40–48 (ca. 475–400)		Nehemiah and Ezra (ca. 475–350)
Joel, Malachi, Proverbs 30–31, Lists (ca. 450)		
JEP redaction [Genesis–Numbers], Isaiah 32–35, Proverbs 1–9, Ruth, Obad (ca. 425)		
JEPD redaction, Jonah, Psalms, Proverbs redaction	400 B.C.E.	The Hellenistic Period (ca. 330–63)
Song of Songs, Chronicles, Ezra, Nehemiah (ca. 400)		
Ecclesiastes (ca. 350)		
Zechariah 9–14 (ca. 325)		

TEXTUAL		HISTORICAL
Isaiah 24–27, Ezekiel 38–39 (ca. 300)	300 B.C.E.	
The Septuagint, a translation of the Hebrew Bible into Greek (ca. 250–100)		
	200 B.C.E.	
		The Maccabean Revolt (ca. 165)
Daniel (ca. 175)		
Esther (ca. 100)	100 B.C.E.	Pompey takes Jerusalem (ca. 63)
	10 B.C.E.	Birth of Christ (ca. 6)
	B.C.E.	
	C.E.	
	C.E. 10	
	C.E. 20	
		Baptism of Christ and the beginning of John's Ministry (ca. 26)
	C.E. 30	Crucifixion of Christ and Pentecost (ca. 30)
		Conversion of Paul (ca. 32)
		Martyrdom of James (ca. 44)
	C.E. 40	Paul and Barnabas visit Jerusalem during famine (ca. 46)
		Paul's First Missionary Journey (ca. 47–48)
Galatians (ca. 49)		Paul's Second Missionary Journey (ca. 49–52)
Thessalonian Letters (ca. 50)	C.E. 50	

125

TEXTUAL		HISTORICAL
Corinthian Letters (ca. 53–55)	C.E. 50	Paul's Third Missionary Journey (ca. 52–56)
Romans (ca. 56)		Paul is arrested in Jerusalem and is imprisoned by Caesar (ca. 56–58)
		Paul's voyage to Rome and shipwreck (ca. 58)
Philippians (ca. 60)	C.E. 60	First Roman imprisonment of Paul (ca. 59–60)
Colossians, Philemon (ca. 61–62)		Paul's release and last travels (ca. 61–63)
Mark (65–67)		Paul's second Roman imprisonment, martyrdom and death (ca. 64–65)
		Death of Peter (ca. 64–65)
Matthew (75–80)	C.E. 70	Fall of Jerusalem (ca. 70)
	C.E. 80	
Canonization of the Hebrew Bible at Synod of Jamnia (ca. 90)	C.E. 90	Persecutions under Emperor Domitian discussed in Revelation (ca. 93–96)
Ephesians, Hebrews, Revelation, Luke, Acts (ca. 95); 1 Peter (ca. 95–100), Fourth Gospel (ca. 95–115)		
Johannine Epistles (ca. 110–115)	C.E. 100	
James, Jude (ca. 125–150)	C.E. 125	
2 Peter (ca. 150)	C.E. 150	
Timothy, Titus (ca. 160–175)		

126

HISTORICAL

TEXTUAL

	C.E. 175	
	C.E. 200	
	C.E. 300	
	C.E. 400	Stabilization of the New Testament canon of twenty-seven books (ca. 350–400)
		Jerome completes the Latin Vulgate, a translation of the Bible based on the Septuagint and translated from the Hebrew (ca. 400)
	C.E. 500	
	C.E. 600	
	C.E. 700	
	C.E. 800	
	C.E. 900	
	C.E. 1000	
	C.E. 1100	
	C.E. 1200	
	C.E. 1300	The first translation of the Bible into English, by John Wycliffe (ca. 1382)
	C.E. 1400	The Gutenburg Bible is printed from movable type, ushering in the new era of printing (1456)
	C.E. 1500	Erasmus finishes a translation of the Bible into Greek (1516)

127

TEXTUAL

Martin Luther translates the Bible into German (1522)	C.E. 1500
William Tyndale and Miles Coverdale's English translations of the Bible (1535)	
Matthew's Bible is produced, based on the Tyndale and Coverdale versions (1537)	
The Great Bible is produced by Coverdale (1539)	
The Geneva Bible, the first to separate chapters into verses (1560)	C.E. 1600
The Douay–Rheims Bible, a Catholic translation from Latin into English (1582–1610)	
The King James Version is completed (1611)	
	C.E. 1700
	C.E. 1800
The English Revised Version is coissued by English and American scholars (1885)	C.E. 1900
The American Standard Version (1901)	
The Moffatt Bible (1924)	
The Smith–Goodspeed Bible (1931)	
The Confraternity Version, an Episcopal revision of the Douay–Rheims Bible (1941)	
Knox's Version, based on the Latin Vulgate and authorized by the Catholic Church (1945–49)	
The Revised Standard Version (1952)	

TEXTUAL

C.E. 1900

The New English Bible, Protestant (1961)
The Jerusalem Bible, Catholic (1966)
The Modern Language Bible (1969)
The New American Bible, Catholic (1970)
Today's English Version (1976)
The New International Version (1978)
The New Jewish Version (1982)

Contributors

HAROLD BLOOM, Sterling Professor of the Humanities at Yale University, is the author of *The Anxiety of Influence*, *Poetry and Repression*, and many other volumes of literary criticism. His forthcoming study, *Freud: Transference and Authority*, attempts a full-scale reading of all of Freud's major writings. A MacArthur Prize Fellow, he is general editor of five series of literary criticism published by Chelsea House. During 1987–88, he was appointed Charles Eliot Norton Professor of Poetry at Harvard University.

SIGMUND FREUD, 1856–1939, was the founder of psychoanalysis and one of the seminal thinkers of our age. A practicing psychoanalyst, he was also Professor of Neurology at the University of Vienna. Freud's studies in human consciousness include, among many others, *Project for a Scientific Psychology*, *The Interpretation of Dreams*, *Jokes and Their Relation to the Unconscious*, *Totem and Taboo*, *Beyond the Pleasure Principle*, *The Ego and the Id*, and *Civilization and Its Discontents*.

MARTIN BUBER is one of the most influential and prolific modern scholars of Judaism and the Hebrew Bible. His best known books include *Moses*, *Israel and Palestine*, and *The Prophetic Faith*.

MICHAEL FISHBANE teaches in the Department of Jewish Religious History at Brandeis University. He is the author of *Text and Texture: Close Readings of Selected Biblical Passages*.

NORTHROP FRYE is University Professor of English at the University of Toronto. His epochal books include *Fearful Symmetry: A Study of William Blake*, and *Anatomy of Criticism*.

MICHAEL WALZER is Professor of Social Science at the Institute of Advanced Study at Princeton. He is the author of *Spheres of Justice*, *Radical Principles*, and *Just and Unjust Wars*.

131

ROBERT ALTER is Professor of Hebrew and Comparative Literature at the University of California, Berkeley. His critical studies include *Defenses of the Imagination* and *Partial Magic: The Novel as a Self-Conscious Genre.*

LESLIE BRISMAN is Professor of English at Yale University. His influential works include *Romantic Origins* and *Milton's Poetry of Choice and Its Romantic Heirs.*

Bibliography

Aberbach, M. and L. Smolar. "Aaron, Jeroboam, and the Golden Calves." *Journal of Biblical Literature* 86 (1967): 129–40.

Ackerman, James. "The Literary Context of the Moses Birth Story." In *Literary Interpretations of Biblical Narratives,* vol. 1, edited by Kenneth R. R. Gros Louis, James Ackerman, and Thayer S. Warshaw. Nashville, Tenn.: Abingdon Press, 1974.

Albright, W. *Yahweh and the Gods of Canaan.* Garden City, N.J.: Doubleday, 1968.

Alt, Albrecht. *Die Ursprunge des israelitischen Rechts.* Leipzig: Hirzel, 1934.

Anderson, B. A. "Exodus Typology in Second Isaiah." In *Israel's Prophetic Heritage,* edited by B. A. Anderson and W. Harrelson. New York: Harper & Row, 1962.

Auerbach, Erich. *Moses.* Amsterdam: G. J. A. Ruys, 1953.

Batto, Bernard F. "Red Sea or Reed Sea: How the Mistake Was Made." *Biblical Archaeology Review* 10, no. 4 (1984): 57–63.

Block, Ernest. *Atheism in Christianity: The Religion of Exodus and the People.* Translated by J. T. Swann. New York: Herder, 1972.

Buber, Martin. *Moses: The Revelation and the Covenant.* New York: Harper and Row, 1958.

———. "What are We to Do about the Ten Commandments?" In *On the Bible: Eighteen Studies by Martin Buber,* edited by Nahum N. Glatzer. New York: Schocken, 1968.

———. "The Words on the Tablets (Exodus 20)." In *On the Bible: Eighteen Studies by Martin Buber,* edited by Nahum N. Glatzer. New York: Schocken, 1968.

Cassuto, Umberto. *Commentary on Exodus.* Jerusalem: Magnus Press, 1965.

Childs, Brevard Springs. *The Book of Exodus.* Philadelphia: Westminster, 1974.

Clements, Ronald E. *Exodus.* Cambridge: Cambridge University Press, 1972.

———. *Prophecy and Covenant.* Naperville, Ill.: A. R. Allenson, 1965.

Coats, George W. *Rebellion in the Wilderness.* Nashville, Tenn.: Abingdon Press, 1968.

———. "The Traditio-Historical Character of the Reed Sea Motif." *Vetus Testamentum* 17 (1967): 253–65.

Croatto, J. Severino. *Exodus: A Hermeneutics of Freedom.* Translated by Salvator Attanasio. Maryknoll, N.Y.: Orbis, 1981.

Cross, Frank Moore. *Canaanite Myth and Hebrew Epic.* Cambridge, Mass.: Harvard University Press, 1973.

Daiches, David. *Moses: The Man and His Vision.* New York: Praeger, 1975.

Damrosch, David. *The Narrative Covenant.* New York: Harper & Row, 1987.

Daube, D. *The Exodus Pattern in the Bible.* London: Faber & Faber, 1963.

Davies, G. I. *The Way of the Wilderness.* Cambridge: Cambridge University Press, 1979.

Dyer, Charles H. "The Date of the Exodus Reexamined." *Bibliotheca Sacra* 140 (1983): 225–43.

Exum, Cheryl. "You Shall Let Every Daughter Live: A Study of Exodus 1:8–2:10." *Semeia* 28 (1983): 63–82.

Finegan, Jack. *Let My People Go: A Journey Through Exodus.* New York: Harper & Row, 1963.

Fishbane, Michael. "The Exodus Motif / The Paradigm of Historical Renewal." In *Text and Texture: Close Readings of Selected Biblical Passages,* 121–40. New York: Schocken, 1979.

Ginzburg, Louis. *The Legends of the Jews.* Translated by Henrietta Szold. Philadelphia: Jewish Publication Society, 1910.

Goldin, Jack. *The Song at the Sea.* New Haven, Conn.: Yale University Press, 1971.

Greenberg, Moshe. "The Redaction of the Plague Narrative in Exodus." In *The Ancient Near East,* edited by H. Goedicke. Baltimore: The Johns Hopkins University Press, 1971.

———. *Understanding Exodus.* New York: Behrman House, 1969.

Gore, Norman C. *Tzeenahu u-reenah: A Jewish Commentary on the Book of Exodus.* New York: Vantage Press, 1965.

Isbell, Charles. "The Structure of Exodus 1:1–14." In *Art and Meaning: Rhetoric in Biblical Literature,* edited by David J. A. Clines, David M. Gunn, and Alan J. Hauser. Sheffield, England: JSOT Press, 1982.

Jacob, Benno. *The Second Book of the Torah.* New York: Ktav, 1987.

Josephus. *The Famous and Memorable Works of Josephus.* Translated by Thomas Lodge. London: 1620.

Leibowitz, Nehama. *Studies in Shemot: The Books of Exodus.* Jerusalem: World Zionist Organization, Department for Torah Education and Culture, 1976.

McCarthy, Dennis. "Moses' Dealings with Pharoh: Exodus 7, 8–10, 27." *Catholic Biblical Quarterly* 27 (1965): 336–47.

———. "Plagues and the Sea of Reeds: Exodus 5–14." *Journal of Biblical Literature* 85 (1966): 137–58.

Mendenhall, George. "Covenant Forms in Israelite Tradition." *Biblical Archaeologist* 17 (1954): 50–76.

Nicholson, Ernest. *Exodus and Sinai in History and Tradition.* Oxford: Basil Blackwell, 1973.

Nohrnberg, James. "Moses." In *Images of Man and God: Old Testament Short Stories in Literary Focus,* edited by Burke O. Long. Sheffield, England: JSOT Press, 1981.

Noth, Martin. *Exodus.* Philadelphia: Westminster, 1962.

Rad, Gerhard von. *Moses.* London: Faber & Faber, 1960.

————. *Old Testament Theology*. New York: Harper & Row, 1962.

Ryken, Leland. "The Epic of Exodus." In *The Literature of the Bible*. Grand Rapids, Mich.: Zondervan Publishing House, 1974.

Sarna, Nahum M. *Exploring Exodus*. New York: Schocken, 1986.

Scholem, Gershom. *The Messianic Idea in Judaism*. New York: Schocken, 1971.

Steffens, Lincoln. *Moses in Red: The Revolt of Israel as a Typical Revolution*. Philadelphia: Dorrance, 1973.

Vogt, Joseph. *Ancient Slavery and the Ideal of Man*. Translated by Thomas Wiedemann. Oxford: Basil/Blackwell, 1974.

Winnet, F. V. *The Mosaic Tradition*. Toronto: University of Toronto Press, 1949.

Acknowledgments

"Moses an Egyptian" (originally entitled "Moses an Egyptian" and "If Moses Was an Egyptian") by Sigmund Freud from *Moses and Monotheism* by Sigmund Freud, © 1939 by Alfred A. Knopf, Inc., © renewed 1967 by Ernest L. Freud and Anna Freud. Reprinted by permission of Alfred A. Knopf, Inc., and Chatto & Windus Ltd.: The Hogarth Press.

"The Burning Bush (Exodus 3)" (originally entitled "The Burning Bush") by Martin Buber from *On the Bible: Eighteen Studies by Martin Buber*, edited by Nahum N. Glatzer, © 1968 by Schocken Books, Inc. Reprinted by permission of Schocken Books, Inc.

"Holy Event (Exodus 19–27)" (originally entitled "Holy Event") by Martin Buber from *On the Bible: Eighteen Studies by Martin Buber*, edited by Nahum N. Glatzer, © 1968 by Schocken Books, Inc. Reprinted by permission of Schocken Books, Inc.

"Exodus 1–4 / The Prologue to the Exodus Cycle" by Michael Fishbane from *Text and Texture: Close Readings of Biblical Texts* by Michael Fishbane, © 1979 by Schocken Books, Inc. Reprinted by permission of Schocken Books, Inc.

"Exodus: The Definitive Deliverance" (originally entitled "Myth II: Narrative") by Northrop Frye from *The Great Code: The Bible and Literature* by Northrop Frye, © 1982 by Northrop Frye. Reprinted by permission of Harcourt Brace Jovanovich, Inc.

"The House of Bondage: Slaves in Egypt" by Michael Walzer from *Exodus and Revolution* by Michael Walzer, © 1985 by Basic Books, Inc. Reprinted by permission of Basic Books, Inc., Publishers and Georges Borchardt, Inc.

"The Song of the Sea" by Robert Alter from *The Art of Biblical Poetry* by Robert Alter, © 1985 by Robert Alter. Reprinted by permission of Basic Books, Inc., Publishers.

"On the Divine Presence in Exodus" by Leslie Brisman, © 1987 by Leslie Brisman. Published for the first time in this volume. Printed by permission.

Index